HISTORIC
CONCORD

and the

LEXINGTON
FIGHT

Leslie Perrin Wilson

HISTORIC

CONCORD
and the LEXINGTON
FIGHT

*A Brief History
of Concord*
BY ALLEN FRENCH

*with an
All-New Guide*
BY LESLIE PERRIN WILSON

PREVIOUS PAGE: *detail from* Central Part of Concord, Mass., *1839, engraving by J. Downes from drawing by John Warner Barber; included in Barber's Historical Collections, 1840. The Barber engraving in full is printed above; the vignette images throughout the book are also from this engraving.*

BOOK DESIGN & PRODUCTION: Reynolds Design & Management, Waltham, Massachusetts

MAP ARTWORK: © 2010 Leslie Evans

TYPEFACE: Sabon

PAPER: Galerie Art Gloss and Anthem Matte and Gloss, 10% post consumer waste, FSC certification

PRINTER: PuritanCapital, Hollis, New Hampshire, www.puritancapital.com

FSC
www.fsc.org
MIX
Paper from
responsible sources
FSC® C006060

DEDICATION

To the people of Concord on the
three hundred and seventy-fifth anniversary
of their town's incorporation,
September 12, 2010

*Humble as is our village in the circle of later
and prouder towns that whiten the land, it has
been consecrated by the presence of the purest
men. . . . But even more sacred influences than
these have mingled here with the stream of
human life. The merit of those who fill a space
in the world's history, who are borne forward,
as it were, by the weight of thousands whom
they lead, sheds a perfume less sweet than do
the sacrifices of private virtue.*

—Ralph Waldo Emerson

*A Historical Discourse, Delivered Before the
Citizens of Concord, 12th September, 1835.
On the Second Centennial Anniversary of the
Incorporation of the Town.*

CONTENTS

PREFACE TO THE 375TH ANNIVERSARY EDITION

WHAT BETTER WAY TO CELEBRATE THE 375TH ANNIVERSARY of the incorporation of Concord than by revisiting the town's history? As part of this celebration, the Friends of the Concord Free Public Library are honored to present a new edition of *Historic Concord and the Lexington Fight* as a birthday present to the town.

What most strikes the reader comparing earlier editions of *Historic Concord* with the present one is how much has changed even when the subject is history. New interpretations, new sites, new vistas abound. Concord's understanding of its history has become better informed, more nuanced, and more accessible. We now approach historic sites not just as places of homage to a single iconic person or event or time period, but rather as layered reflections of social history. The visitor is encouraged to explore the stories—the daily lives and dramas—of the many occupants of a historic home over time. History incorporates narratives of geological periods, of Pre-contact life, and of land use and change as well as more traditional narratives of "important" events.

As understanding of Concord's history has evolved, so has its presentation in the several editions of *Historic Concord*. The earliest version was a brief historical pamphlet written by Allen French—historian, writer of historical fiction, and Concord resident—and published in 1924 as a John Hancock Mutual Life Insurance Company booklet. It focused on Concord as a Revolutionary site and home to eminent nineteenth-century American authors. French reworked this pamphlet into the 1942 first edition of the book in the history-cum-guidebook format that has been retained to the present time. Lexington's role on that fateful April morning in 1775 was more explicitly acknowledged in the title, the historical narrative, and the separate Guide section than in the preceding history. Lester Hornby's graceful illustrations were first included in the 1942 edition.

In 1978, David Little—a museum registrar and local historian who had grown up in Concord—expanded the book for the Friends of the Concord Free Public Library, making it substantially more useful as a practical guidebook while still retaining French's short history. In his 1992 revised edition, Little further expanded the Guide section, added supplementary material, and introduced some historical images from the Concord Free Public Library Special Collections. He also drew attention to Concord's need for a better Visitor Center to promote formal and consistent interpretation of local sites (finally realized in 2002).

It has been almost twenty years since the last revision of *Historic Concord*. The Friends of the Library have been fortunate in engaging a knowledgeable writer on Concord's history to revise and update the new edition of this book. Leslie Perrin Wilson has curated and directed the Library's Special Collections since 1996 and is the author of *In History's Embrace,* a consideration of the role Concord's history has played in shaping life here. In the 375th anniversary edition of *Historic Concord,* Wilson has replaced Hornby's illustrations with an outstanding selection of historical images from the Concord Free Public Library Special Collections. In addition, she has expanded the Guide section to include more sites and more context and detail about some sites, while making this section easier to use.

Whether you are a visitor to or a resident of Concord, we hope that you will enjoy *Historic Concord* and gain new insights into this unique and special place.

Barbara A. Powell, *Librarian Emerita*
Concord Free Public Library, Concord, Massachusetts

HISTORY

*A Brief Sketch
of Concord's First
Two Hundred and Fifty Years,
1635–1885,
Including an Account
of the Lexington Fight*

BY ALLEN FRENCH

*As published in 1942
and later reprinted*

Central Part of
Concord, Mass.,
*1839, detail from
engraving by
J. Downes from
drawing by John
Warner Barber;
included in
Barber's* Historical
Collections, *1840*

THE COLONIAL PERIOD

CONCORD'S HISTORY DIVIDES ITSELF NATURALLY into three periods: the founding, with the early struggles to survive; the Revolutionary, with the reason for and the facts of the Concord Fight; and the literary, with the local story of some of the country's greatest writers. These follow each other in order of time but in the same scene, for Emerson walked where his ancestor Bulkeley made the treaty with the Indians, and Hawthorne dwelt but two hundred yards from the North Bridge. It is worth noting that through the whole story the geography of the town connects itself with the events of its history.

Where a little stream, centuries ago, ran straight through level land, the Indians made a fishweir to trap the spring run of shad and herring. On broad meadows, farther away, they cultivated, here and there, patches of maize. On two rivers which joined and made one they paddled their canoes, and along the banks they hunted waterfowl. A certain ridge which entered their territory from the east, and twice turned till it ran northerly, probably was of no use to them. So too with the three hills which rose from the plain, unless their woods could be hunted for game. At one spot the Indians held their feasts of river clams, and the shells remain to tell of it.[1] At others the savages made and abandoned and made again their cobbled fireplaces.[2] If the region was the scene of Indian warfare, there is no record of it. But where they hunted they lost their arrowheads, and where they worked they left their mortars and pestles, axes and awls. They still occupied the area in 1635, and to this day the soil renders up the stone tools that tell of them.

When white men came they saw that the brook, if dammed, would run a mill. The rivers were unimportant: they led to the wrong place by the sea.[3] But the meadows they liked, especially those spots where Indian hoes and clearance fires had prepared the way for better cultivation. (The English had yet to learn that the rivers would overflow the lower spots.) And the ridge would be of use, for it would hold their meeting house and their homes in a place suited for defense. So they bargained for a six-mile square, and built the church and dam and dwellings, poor houses, half dugouts in the hillside.[4] Their first road began at a spot, at the first rise of the ridge, where many years later would begin the running fight with the retreating British. Following on below the ridge, the road passed the place where one day would be bred the Concord Grape, and others where yet would dwell the Alcotts, Hawthorne, and Emerson. The road turned a corner, and running straight for awhile, passed the future sites of the best pre-Revolutionary houses, of the church of the original parish, and of the Town House in what is now the Square.

Again the road turned, and seeking a site to cross the river, found one that was used for many years, where the British met their first defeat. All this is still the main artery and the heart of modern Concord. It is true that other important places in Concord lie farther away, also that many changes have occurred. The mill pond is gone, and the mill brook is all but hidden. But the old dam, now a busy street, is still called the Mill Dam; and the simple geography of plain and brook and ridge still influence the daily ways of man.

The first man to map the region was William Wood, who did it crudely in his book of 1634. Probably the first to examine the place with an eye to settling was Simon Willard, "Kentish soldier," who came to the colony in the same year. A fur trader, he doubtless learned of the place from the Indians, and led here the group of "planters." Chief among these were the ministers, Peter Bulkeley and John Jones, both "silenced" in England for their Puritanism. Their families, and those that accompanied them, amounted to perhaps sixty-five in all. The founders bore names long known in Concord history: Hosmer, Buttrick, Hunt, Ball, Meriam, Flint, and still others. Their grant from the General Court was dated September 12, 1635.

An equally necessary step was the treaty with the Indians. Tradition says that it took place under a great tree, the site of which is still marked on the Square. The white men "on the one party, and Squaw Sachem, Tahattawan, Nimrod, Indians, on the other party," came to an agreement. The white men gave tools, knives, cloth, and shirts, and fitted out the medicine man, husband to the female sachem, with "a suit of cotton cloth, an hat, a white linen band, shoes, stockings, and a great coat." Then "Mr. Simon Willard, pointing to the four quarters of the world, declared that they had bought three miles from that place, east, west, north, and south; and the said Indians manifested their free consent thereunto."

It was this free consent of the Indians, some have said, that gave the name of Concord to the town. Others, however, have believed that the name, first mentioned in the Boston grant, signified the perfect agreement among the settlers themselves. At any rate, in the summer of 1636 their crops were planted on the meadows, and their first crude houses were completed, not far from the equally simple church which stood on the ridge above the present Square.

Life in Concord during its first years was hard. Bulkeley had brought money with him, and established various members of the town on farms, cutting down his own resources. But the soil was harsh and the trees many; wolves ate the swine; the meadows flooded; and most of the settlers were unskilled in the new life. They "cut their bread very thin for a long season," said their historian. "Thus this poore people populate this howling Desart." They felt their isolation, being the only ones away from tidewater, miles from the nearest whites, and fearful of the savages. At length some of them, led by the minister Jones, went away to Connecticut, leaving Bulkeley and the remainder more lonely still. It was only after another few years that Concord began to prosper.

Fear of the Indians, freely admitted by the settlers, was not justified in these earliest times. The tribesmen of that generation helped the settlers, bringing them game, and teaching them how to plant the Indian corn with a few herring, caught in the spring run, in every hill as fertilizer. It was not until 1675 that the fear of Indians was justified. Then Metacomet, "King Philip," led the Indians against the whites. One raid came too near the town, when the two brothers Shepard, working their farm in what is now Littleton, were ambushed and slain, and their sister Mary carried off. She escaped, however, and came to Concord with the alarm. Concord men were in the famous fight at Brookfield, where various of them were killed, and where Capt. Thomas Wheeler was brought out of the skirmish by his son Thomas, both of them wounded. The party, besieged in a house, was at length rescued by men under Simon Willard, then in his old age.

Concord village was spared an attack by the reputation of its pastor, Edward Bulkeley, for when the Indians consulted whether the town should be raided, a chief declared, "We no prosper, if we go to Concord. The Great Spirit love that people—they have a great man there—he great pray!"

Two incidents during this war give honor, if not to Concord, at least to one of its citizens. Among the Indians there were converts to Christianity, who remained peaceful while their tribe went to war. Yet they were under strong suspicion by the whites; therefore to keep them from either doing or receiving harm, they were brought together in Concord by John Hoar, who housed them and built them a workshop on his own land, where now stands the Orchard House of the Alcotts. Feeling against them ran high, however; Hoar's humanity and protection were thought not to be enough. The Indians were taken from him by the forceful intervention of soldiers and herded together on an island in Boston Harbor, where they suffered much hardship till the end of the war.

Hoar's spirit was better appreciated, however, when a new need arose. The Indians raided Lancaster, and carried away Mrs. Rowlandson, the wife of the minister. It was believed that she could be ransomed; yet no one dared to go among the Indians with the money until Hoar offered to go. He went, was received with hatred and threats, yet his steady courage brought success, and he returned with the woman.

The peace which followed King Philip's War was presently disturbed by the coming of Governor Andros, who expressed doubt as to the citizens' titles to their land. To satisfy him were made the depositions as to Concord's bargain with the Indians from which we have already quoted. Yet to the protests of various towns Andros declared that he valued an Indian's mark upon their treaties no more than the scratch of a bear's claw. Chiefly for this the colony rose against him, seizing the opportunity offered by the news that in England William of Orange had landed to expel King James. In this little revolt Concord took its share, on the first of the town's three historic Nineteenths of April. On that day, in 1689, Concord's company was mustered in the Square, and marched to Boston to take its part in the imprisonment of Andros.

In England, William was successful; yet he brought to an end one period of Massachusetts history. Believing the colony to be too independent, he changed its form of government. From a colony it became a province, with stricter supervision from the mother country. Under the new charter Massachusetts flourished; there were other wars, but more distant. And Concord was peaceful and prosperous until there loomed the struggle against England itself.

THE REVOLUTIONARY PERIOD

THE STAMP ACT OF 1765 made no outward disturbance in Concord, but by it the minds of the townspeople must have been prepared for further trouble. For the tea controversy, on the question of taxation, brought from the town in 1774 the declaration, characteristic of the times, that while the people would risk their fortunes and lives in defense of the king, they would equally risk them in defense of their charter rights. But the king's authority and the people's liberties proved to be deeply opposed. The town entered wholeheartedly into the struggle against new laws; its meeting house held the earliest sittings of the First Provincial Congress; and when the province began to gather munitions for an army, Concord became the most important storehouse for those means of war. Cannon and their carriages, powder, bullets, camp kettles, and other necessaries were assembled in the town. The Massachusetts leaders believed that in such a patriotic place these stores could be safely kept; and it was for this reason that Concord, and Lexington on the road to Concord, saw the opening scenes of the Revolutionary War.

Perhaps because of its responsibility for the stores, Concord was earlier than most towns in organizing the minute men. These were the younger and more active men from among the old organization of the militia of the province; the two companies were enrolled in January 1775. There were two militia companies as well, with the Alarm Company, composed of old men and boys; but the minute men were pledged to be ready at a minute's warning. So literally did they take this promise that they carried their guns with them to church and to the field.

The minute men companies of the neighboring towns were organized into a regiment of which John Buttrick of Concord was major. Similarly the militia companies were formed into a regiment of which James Barrett of Concord was colonel. Barrett, the older man, had retired from military duties; but he was recalled. Slow and unwieldy on foot, he was still able to ride his horse, as he proved when occasion demanded.

Through the winter the companies of all the neighboring towns drilled at home and met occasionally in musters. A British officer sent out by General Gage, the British governor in Boston, reported these "trainings" with much ridicule, little thinking that he himself would someday retreat before the homespuns.

Every act of either side drew both parties toward war. The governor and his troops were practically cooped up in Boston. Each practice march that the soldiers made into the country was jealously watched, lest one should be made in earnest. Nothing that Gage did could long be kept a secret from the Boston patriots. Nor could the actions of the provincials be kept entirely secret from the governor. He knew that stores were being assembled in Concord, and that an army was being formed against him. It was only common sense for him to destroy the stores if he could, to make the army helpless. Realizing this, the Committee of Safety, when it held in April its sessions in Concord, required Colonel Barrett to keep men and teams ready, by day or night, on the shortest notice to remove the stores. Then, as if knowing that the emergency was at hand, on the eighteenth the committee ordered the removal of many of the stores to towns farther away. And that very night the work began, although no warning had come that in Boston the British expedition was on the move.

For General Gage had at last made up his mind to act. A good administrator, his patience and tact had been great; but he had lost various chances to seize the Massachusetts leaders, and even now he merely tried to take or destroy the stores. He had made no effort to lay hands on Dr. Joseph Warren, openly living in Boston, and the most active man there in watching and blocking the British moves. The mechanics and craftsmen in Boston spied narrowly on all that was done, and brought the news to Warren. And their reports on the night of the "eighteenth of April, in seventy-five," were that troops were on the move, assembling at the foot of the Common, not far from which it was already known that the rowboats of the men-of-war had been moored in waiting. Warren sent for two messengers, both of whom were experienced in riding post for the Committee of Safety.

One of these was William Dawes, whom Warren instructed to attempt to leave Boston by the only land exit, to Roxbury. But as soldiers held the Neck, and Dawes might not be allowed to go out on a night when some movement was in progress, Warren also sent for Paul Revere.

Revere was silversmith and engraver, craftsman extraordinary, and also a patriotic messenger on various occasions. He had lately been to Concord with a message from Warren, and on that occasion had prepared for this very emergency. To Concord, of course, both he and Dawes were sent: it could be the only objective of a secret expedition of the troops. With instructions from Warren, Revere put his plan into execution. Against British orders, he had a hidden boat; but lest he fail in his attempt to leave the town, he sent a friend to signal patriots in Charlestown, across the river, that the troops were leaving Boston by boat. The signal was two lanterns hung in the steeple of the North Church. One of those lanterns is now to be seen in Concord, at the Concord Museum.

Revere succeeded in crossing; though there was light from a young moon, he was not seen by warships or British patrols, and on the Charlestown shore he found friends awaiting him. On Deacon Larkin's horse he rode away on his errand. He took the most direct route, toward Cambridge; but blocked by British mounted officers, whom he saw in the moonlight, he turned back, gave them the slip, and galloped to Medford. From there, and as far as Lexington, he roused every important household on the route.

Lexington

Until three days before, the Provincial Congress had been sitting at Concord, with its two chief members, John Hancock and Samuel Adams, directing every move.[5] On the night of the eighteenth the two were sleeping at the house of the Reverend Jonas Clarke, in Lexington, with a guard of minute men outside.[6] When Revere arrived, about midnight, the sergeant asked Revere to make no noise. "Noise!" he rejoined. "You'll have noise enough before long. The regulars are coming out!"

The town was immediately roused. Hancock and Adams rose and dressed; but while Hancock wished to stay and fight, his wiser companion tried to persuade him to go away.

The minute man company assembled, and under its captain, John Parker, mustered on the Green. Then there was a long waiting. Dawes arrived, and he and Revere set out for Concord, accompanied by young Dr. Samuel Prescott, a Concord man who fortunately happened to be courting his sweetheart in Lexington that night. For when the three met suddenly a second patrol of British officers, Revere was taken and held, Dawes turned back toward Boston, and Prescott alone, escaping by jumping his horse over a wall, roused the captain of the Lincoln minute men, and himself brought the news to Concord.

The Lexington company, mustered on the Green in a night that was moderately cold, received no news from the scouts that they sent down the Boston road. At length their captain dismissed them to houses nearby, and to the Buckman Tavern, almost on the Green, to assemble instantly on the first summons.

Dawn began to break, a chilly morning, when Revere appeared again. His captors, recognizing him, had questioned him, and he had bluffed them with the story that the whole country was in arms and ready for the approaching expedition, of which, to their surprise, he appeared to have accurate news. To warn the expected column, these officers hurried to the Boston road, releasing all their prisoners. Revere hastened back to Lexington and told his story to Hancock and Adams, who quickened their departure. Revere followed them with a trunk of Hancock's papers, which he took to a place of safety. Returning once more, he was just in time to observe what happened on the Green.

The detachment which Gage sent out from Boston numbered probably about seven hundred men, consisting of the grenadier and light infantry companies of all the regiments in Boston. They were therefore unaccustomed to acting together, and not used to their superior officers. These were Lt. Col. Francis Smith of the Tenth Regiment, and Maj. John Pitcairn of the marines. Pitcairn was a steady and sensible officer, not unpopular even with the patriots of Boston. But Smith was heavy, dull, and slow, good for routine duties, but unfitted for an expedition requiring enterprise and initiative.

Blunder after blunder caused delay after delay. The troops mustered late in the evening, but it was some time before they were in their boats, of which there were not enough. Two trips were required to ferry them across the Back Bay and to Lechmere Point in Cambridge. Then there was a long wait for their rations, some of which the men threw away as the food grew heavy on the march. Wet to the knees, the men at length began their journey from the marshes; then they went fast. In the very early morning they passed through the outskirts of Cambridge and through Menotomy, now Arlington. Various stories are told of incidents on the way, but nothing happened to stop the troops until they neared Lexington. They met the scouts who had been sent from Lexington for news. But the British advance patrol, marching silently on the sides of the road, made prisoners of them, and the troops marched on. The light infantry were in the lead, under command of Major Pitcairn.

Now came to warn them the mounted officers who had earlier captured Revere. Pitcairn, halting his troops and consulting, also received the statement that an American had attempted to fire at Lieutenant Sutherland, scouting in front. The major therefore ordered the troops to prime and load, and to march on, "but on no account to Fire, or even attempt it without orders." And so the troops moved forward, entered the village of Lexington, and approached the Green.

Meanwhile, the Americans had received their final alarm.[7] Thaddeus Bowman, scouting to find why no further news of the British had come, was warned by his skittish horse, which shied at the advance picket of the British, and enabled him to see, beyond them, the head of the marching column. Galloping back, he brought the news to the Lexington captain. The drum was beat, and the minute men came running to the Green. Their sergeant formed them in two lines. There were perhaps eighty of them, drawn up in full view of the Concord road, by which the British were expected to pass. It was sunrise, and long shadows fell across the Green.

Perhaps then Parker uttered the words credited to him: "Stand your ground; don't fire unless fired upon; but if they mean to have a war, let it begin here!"[8] Strong words, and suited to a desperate situation; but here was one in which the minute men, parading without defense, invited annihilation from a force many times their number. Months of inaction had fretted the regulars; they were exasperated by the provocations given by the Yankees. If the Lexington men, drawn up where they had a right to be, had expected the troops to pass by on their mission, they were mistaken. The head of the column swerved, entered the Green, and marched directly toward them.

The Lexington church stood then on the Green, on the corner nearest Boston. The column passed on one side; and Pitcairn, seeing what was happening, spurred his horse around the other, to take a position where he could command both the troops and the militia. Various mounted officers were with him.

And Parker saw the unwelcome necessity of the situation. His men could not stand against so many. He gave the order "to disperse and not to fire." Slowly and unwillingly his men began to break ranks.

What happened then is not, and probably never will be, clear. Eyewitnesses on both sides disagree: each said the other fired first. The evidence cannot be reconciled. No doubt Pitcairn uttered the words long imputed to him: "Disperse, ye rebels! Lay down your arms and disperse!" But he solemnly asserted that he ordered his own men not to fire, and tried to prevent it. But his men were eager for the prey so helpless before them. Paul Revere, just then coming within sight of the Green, declared that the first shot fired was from a pistol. Others said the same. Now, in all likelihood the only pistols there were in the hands of the mounted officers, and some were young and hotheaded. However it happened, a shot was fired, then others, and then the advance company fired their guns and rushed in with their bayonets.

Some Americans fell dead on the spot. Others, mortally wounded, dragged themselves away—like Jonathan Harrington, who reached his own doorstep to die at his wife's feet. And still others, fiercely resisting, were bayoneted where they stood—like Jonas Parker, killed while trying to reload.

For the Americans returned the fire, from the Green and from the tavern. In the excitement and the smoke they did but little damage: Pitcairn's horse was hurt, and one of the regulars. But the British possessed the ground, and drove from it the remaining minute men. Eight of the Americans were killed, ten wounded.

The troops, if unrestrained, might have broken into the tavern, the church, and the nearby houses, bayoneting all that they found. But Pitcairn and his officers, and Smith who now arrived, quieted the men. They were formed again, admonished, and ordered to the road. It could not have been half an hour before they were gone, and the men and women of Lexington flocked to the scene, to take up the dead and to care for the wounded.

The townsmen were not cowed. The British had cheered before they marched away. But they would have to come back by that very road, and the men of Lexington prepared for a second encounter, when they could take vengeance for their losses.

Concord

Of all that had happened Concord knew nothing. Young Dr. Prescott had arrived long before dawn, with Revere's tidings. Longfellow was wrong when he wrote in his poem that Revere "came to the bridge in Concord town." Only Prescott's warning came to the town; and so the men in authority, wishing like those in Lexington to learn whether anything was really going to happen, while they still kept on with the hiding of stores, sent a man to Lexington to bring back news.

This was Reuben Brown, harness maker, whose house still stands on Lexington Road. Mounted, he rode to Lexington to find what might be happening. And he arrived at the Green just when the rattle of the British guns rang out, and when smoke enveloped the scene. Bullets whistled; perhaps one came near Brown; and he might have seen the head of the column of grenadiers, advancing on the Boston road. Brown thought he had seen enough, and turned and galloped back.

But Major Buttrick was not satisfied. He asked if the British had fired with ball. Brown's answer is quaintly delicious. "I do not know, but think it probable." Buttrick doubtless drew his conclusions; yet action proceeded on the assumption that the militia must not fire first.

As time passed and still the British did not appear, the minute man companies were sent down Lexington Road to reconnoiter. They had reached the end of the ridge, at Meriam's Corner, when across the level ground they saw the British column descending the opposite slope. The regulars were so superior in force that the minute men marched back and reported to the field officers, waiting with the militia on the ridge opposite the meeting house. It was wise to depart and wait for reinforcements. The little force, consisting of the Concord and Lincoln companies, marched to another height overlooking the road to the North Bridge; here Joseph Hosmer was appointed adjutant and the whole put in order. The minister, William Emerson, urged that the place be held: "Let us stand our ground; if we die, let us die here." But wiser counsels prevailed: the provincials were too few. As the British were seen again, marching toward the bridge, the Americans once more retreated before them.

Two men quitted their posts in the line, leaving the ranks as they passed their own houses, to stay with their families and defend them. One was Elisha Jones: his house is now known as the House with the Bullet Hole. The other man was the minister himself, going to the Manse, where were not only his family, but also the wives and children of some of his parishioners. Jones kept himself out of sight. His house contained a number of barrels of beef, with salt fish and other stores, but it was not entered. Neither were the Manse grounds, where the minister, ignoring his wife's entreaties to come indoors, remained outside with his people, watching what happened at the bridge and on the roads.

On their arrival the British had taken possession of the center of the town. Smith and Pitcairn made their headquarters at the Wright Tavern, and they sent out parties to search for munitions. Two large brass cannon, twenty-four pounders, were discovered at the Jones Tavern.[9] The exulting British spiked them and knocked off their trunnions. With the same feeling, the troops cut down the Liberty Pole, which was on the ridge. Bullets were found and thrown into the millpond, and barrels of flour were also rolled into the water. But later the Americans dragged out both bullets and barrels, when it was found that the barrels had swelled, and only the outer part of the flour had been damaged. No powder was found, nor many of the important stores, for the Yankees turned aside the search of the British by one pretense or another.

Thus in Timothy Wheeler's barn were stored many barrels of flour belonging to the province, together with others of his own. He readily admitted the British searching party and showed the barrels. "This," he said, pointing to his own property, "is my own. I am a miller, sir. Yonder stands my mill. This is my wheat; this is my rye; this is mine." "Well," said the officer, "we do not injure private property." And he withdrew with his men.

The officers, therefore, were humane, and their men under control. Some of the soldiers, trying to get information from old Deacon Thomas Barrett, threatened him with death as a rebel. He remonstrated mildly: they might save themselves the trouble, for he would soon die of himself. "Well, old daddy," they replied, "you may go in peace," and they released him.

Yet there was plenty of excitement in the town. One woman, as if to receive company, put on one fresh apron after another until she was wearing seven. Her neighbor, wiser, rescued from the church the

Communion silver and put it in the soft-soap barrel in the Wright Tavern. When taken out next day, it was pot-black.

The excitement grew when cannon carriages which had been found were burned near the Town House. Martha Moulton, "widow-woman," went to the tavern and begged Pitcairn to extinguish the fire. The officers said good-naturedly, "O, mother, we won't do you any harm. Don't be concerned, mother." But she persisted, and they sent and extinguished the fire which threatened the building.

It is the more difficult, therefore, to ascribe to Pitcairn ("a good man in a bad cause," wrote the patriot Ezra Stiles) the story that at the tavern he stirred his toddy with his finger, and boasted that thus he would stir the Yankee blood that day. Smith, well known as the opposite kind of man, was dull enough not to see the situation that he had put himself in. More than to anyone else, the story belongs to him.

In spite of all care, a fire was started in Reuben Brown's harness shop. It was soon put out. More deliberate was the burning in the Square. The smoke of these fires was seen by the militia beyond the town, and led to action, as we shall see.

Some detachments of the regulars were sent farther away. One company was sent to the South Bridge, and, preventing passage there, searched houses in the neighborhood. A second detachment was sent to the North Bridge. The British knew that some two miles beyond the bridge was the home of Colonel Barrett, where many supplies had been stored. Six companies of light infantry, under Captain Parsons, were therefore sent on a search. Leaving half of them at the bridge to secure his retreat, Parsons went on with the rest. He did not particularly notice that, as he approached, a man was seen plowing in a field—the only man seen peacefully occupied that day. Nor did any of the British guess that cannon were lying in a furrow, and the man was plowing earth over them.

At the house the search produced no great results. Much had been carried away or concealed. Open barrels in the attic, topped with feathers, hid bullets, flints, and even cartridges; but the soldiers did not suspect. More cannon wheels were found, however. When it was proposed to burn them on the spot, and Mrs. Barrett remonstrated for the sake of the barn, they were burned in the road. She refused to take money for food, saying, "We are commanded to feed our enemies."

When officers threw the money in her unwilling lap she said, "This is the price of blood." And when she refused liquor to the men the officers sustained her, saying that they had killed men at Lexington, and more bloody work was sure to follow.

Meanwhile Captain Laurie, in command of the companies at the bridge, posted them across it, one at the bridgehead and two on the hillsides beyond, to watch and prevent any movement by the Americans. These had retreated to Punkatasset Hill, a mile farther away, where slowly reinforcements came in—the Bedford and Acton companies, the smaller one from little Carlisle, nearby, and men singly or in groups from Chelmsford, Westford, and Littleton. Concord men returning from hiding the supplies joined their companies. And as the force grew in numbers, and anxiety for the town increased, they marched down again to a spot overlooking the bridge, where for a time the British below watched them with interest and suspicion.

Hosmer put the companies in line, the minute men on the right, the militia on the left. Barrett, who had been very busy all the morning on horseback, was now on the ground, with Buttrick and the selectmen. It used to be said that the men were ordered to discard all doubtful gunflints,[10] to make sure of an effective fire. This tale was proved true only a few years ago, when nearly a hundred gunflints were found in the field, an unusual number that can only have come from the one cause.

As the men looked in the direction of the town, they saw smoke rising from it in new and greater quantities. It looked as if the town were on fire. And Hosmer, alarmed and indignant, went at once to the group of older men. Breaking into their consultation, he pointed to the smoke and asked the question, now historic, "Will you let them burn the town down?"

The decision was immediate: to march into the town, or die in its defense. Colonel Barrett gave the order for the troops to march. But on no account were they to fire first. The two British companies on the hillsides below saw that the provincials were too strong for them, and marched back to join the third one at the bridge. Lieutenant Sutherland, whom we have seen near Lexington, had come with the British as a volunteer. Impatient for something to happen, he was just starting for the Barrett farm; but thinking that "it would be disgracefull to be taken by such Rascals," he too went to the bridge. Here Laurie waited long enough to perceive that his own position was not safe. Therefore he marched his three companies across the bridge; then strangely, quite forgetful of Parsons two miles away, he ordered men out upon the bridge to take up the planks. Sutherland, eager to be of use, undertook to supervise the work.

On roads recently restored by the National Park Service, the Americans marched down the hill, then, turning a corner, marched directly at the bridge. Buttrick was leading, and by his side, as aide, marched Lieutenant Colonel Robinson of Westford. First in line behind them came the Acton company, whose captain, Isaac Davis, had said as he accepted the post, "I haven't a man that's afraid to go." The Concord minute man companies followed, and then the remaining minute men and militia, even down to the Concord Alarm Company of old men and half-grown boys. They marched two-and-two, perhaps four hundred in all, and their fifes played the stirring tune of the "White Cockade."

As they approached the bridge, Buttrick shouted to the soldiers taking up the planks, ordering them to "desist." They quitted the spot just as Laurie, to make his fire more effective, ordered men into the fields to right and left of the bridge, ready to fire on the advancing Americans. Only one officer obeyed the order: Sutherland, who took two men with him into the Manse field.

Above and behind him, the minister, Emerson, stood at the height of his own land, anxiously watching everything that happened.

In warning, next, the British fired a few shots into the river, and then another directly at the Americans. The ball passed under Robinson's arm and wounded an Acton and a Concord man. The Americans marched steadily on. Buttrick cannot have been far from the bridge, with the Acton men close behind, when the front ranks of the regulars fired their volley. It killed the Acton captain and one of his men, and wounded others in the ranks. One man, cut by a bullet, cried out that the British were firing jackknives.

Buttrick, leaping into the air as he turned to his men, shouted, "Fire, fellow-soldiers, for God's sake, fire!" The word was passed; the front ranks fired; and men behind them broke from the ranks to fire at the British. Then all surged forward to take the bridge.

A few more British shots may have been fired, but in haste, and harmless. And the regulars broke. Four of their officers, out of eight, were wounded, among them Sutherland in the field. A sergeant was hit; two men were killed; another was mortally wounded; and several were hurt. The remainder (there were but a hundred and twenty men at most) saw Buttrick and the Acton men already on the bridge. And so they ran, carrying with them their officers and the few veterans who would have held them. In that minute or two the Concord Fight was over.

This was Concord's share in beginning the Revolution—attack, no longer defense. It was heroic. These men knew the law: no people could have studied the situation better. They knew the penalty of rebellion, of failure. They had every reason to fear trained soldiers better armed than themselves. But protecting their homes, and at last defying their king, they struck to make themselves free.

There was one further incident. As the straggling British passed the house of Elisha Jones, its owner rashly showed himself in the doorway of the ell, his gun in his hand. Some regular with gun still loaded, angry and glad of the mark, fired at him. The shot went wide—its hole is still to be seen, about three feet to the left of where Jones stood. The soldiers passed on, and Jones wisely put himself out of sight. But the bullet hole remains to tell the story.

Like most militia, the Americans were disorganized by their success. Some took up their dead and wounded; others rallied, and marching forward, saw a reinforcement of grenadiers approaching from the village, and took post behind walls. Forgetful of Parsons, still beyond the bridge, Smith, who led the grenadiers, halted and marched them back. The provincials also forgot, and Parsons led his men in safety to the village. The Fight had happened a little before ten o'clock. It was not until about noon that Smith, wasting valuable time as he tended his wounded, marched for Boston. Equally wasteful of their time, the Americans watched and waited for any movement that Smith might make. They did not block the roads, but were merely ready to fight again. Sudbury and Framingham men came to the ground, and all were prepared to strike the British.

Smith made a good disposition as he left the town. His wounded were in commandeered chaises on the road, guarded by the grenadiers.

To right and left, on the meadows and the ridge, the light infantry flanked the little column. (On the ridge, readers of Hawthorne may recall, the writer set the scene of the duel between the British officer and Septimius Felton.) A mile from town the British reached Meriam's Corner again. And there began the famous running fight. All the way to Lexington the militia, fighting without order, every man for himself, took post behind any shelter (sometimes, forgetting the British flankers, too close) and fired at the retreating regulars, giving them no time to form, and no object at which to charge. As the British approached Lexington, the men of that town were ready and took their revenge.

Yet there the regulars, tired and with empty guns, met safety. Smith's one wise action of the day was in the early morning, when he sent to Gage to ask support. And now in Lexington Lord Percy's brigade came to save him, having with it two fieldpieces which awed the militia more than all the muskets. Under this protection the fugitives rested awhile; then the two detachments marched back to Boston. They were harried all the way by more and more provincials, they lost both men and pride; but they gave as well as took, for many Americans, venturing too close, learned that the redcoats still could strike. And the regulars made good their retreat. Late in the day the wearied remainder reached Charlestown in safety, and were ferried across the Charles (which Revere had crossed by the light of the moon) to the rest and comfort of their barracks. But that very night the Americans closed in around Boston, and began the siege which after eleven months, under Washington, drove the British from the town.

Only four Concord men (three of them captains) were wounded on that day. Concord soldiers took part in the Siege of Boston. Since Cambridge was occupied by the American troops, Harvard College removed to Concord, and remained through an academic year. Classes were held in the meeting house, and in private houses. College Lane, a little-used highway at the western end of the town, is today the only reminder of that episode. Yet three members of the class which graduated here returned to stay: Jonathan Fay, lawyer in the town for thirty-three years; Dr. Hurd, who practiced here for fifty-five years; and Ezra Ripley, for sixty-three years minister.

In the disturbed period after the Revolution, Concord was once more the scene of rebellious activity, this time largely by old soldiers against the very government which they had defended. Great public burdens, high taxes, business depression, bad money, and imprisonment for debt of men who had served the country were the grievances. In September 1786, Job Shattuck and two to three hundred men, as a part of the now almost forgotten "rebellion" of Daniel Shays, took possession of Concord Square, closed the courthouse, forbade the courts to sit, and petitioned for redress. The little uprising, which ended in dispersion of the shabby muster, nevertheless had a good influence in hastening Massachusetts's acceptance of the new Federal Constitution.

The Concord Fight was the town's one direct experience of war, yet Concord men have always been ready to serve. As the Fight occurred just eighty-six years to a day after the town's militia marched out against Andros, so after another eighty-six years, on another Nineteenth of April, Concord's company marched to the Civil War. They have fought in all wars since. The four monuments on the Square, and the beautiful Melvin Memorial in Sleepy Hollow, testify to the devotion of Concord men.

CONCORD IN LITERATURE

BY A CURIOUS CHANCE, Concord's literary story is linked with its earlier fame. William Emerson, the fiery minister, acted as chaplain in the Revolution, and died of camp fever. His son, also William, lived as minister in Boston, but died almost equally young. Meanwhile Ezra Ripley, successor to the first William, married the widow, and lived in the Manse. He was helpful to his step grandchildren, sometimes housed the family, and said once to Ralph Waldo Emerson, "I wish you and your brothers to come to this house as you have always done. You will not like to be excluded; I shall not like to be neglected." It was this influence which made Emerson so much of a Concordian. In the town where his ancestors had lived (for he was a descendant of three of Concord's ministers) he himself came to dwell. And it was Emerson's influence which brought the Alcotts here, to some extent Hawthorne as well, and helped to develop the genius of Thoreau, a native of the town. Others, such as Margaret Fuller, Channing the poet, George William Curtis, came and went; but these—living, writing, dying, and buried in Concord—were Concord's literary group.

Emerson

Ralph Waldo Emerson, born in Boston in 1803, was often in Concord in his youth, but did not come here to live until 1834. Meanwhile he had been a minister, but resigned his work because he could no longer follow the old forms. He had struggled with ill health; he had married, but was a widower. He and his mother first boarded at the Manse. His brother Charles was also in the town, where lived likewise his eccentric aunt, Mary Moody Emerson, she who, born in 1774, used to boast that she was "in arms" at the Concord Fight, and whose oddities did much to conceal her strong good sense and high ambition for her nephews. Emerson wrote for her tombstone, "She gave high counsels." And he lived up to them. Coming to Concord to live, he wrote: "Hail to the quiet fields of my fathers . . . Henceforth I design not to utter any speech, poem, or book that is not entirely and peculiarly my work." He never swerved from that plan. Writing in the field of religion, morals, and social ethics, where thousands had worked before him, he struck out a new line of thought which helped to mold his generation and which influences America to this day.

In 1835 Emerson married Miss Lydia Jackson of Plymouth (whose name he changed to Lidian for the sake of euphony), and bought for his residence the house at the beginning of the Cambridge Turnpike. Here his children were born; and here he lived for nearly fifty years, until his death in 1882. His habits were simple. Daily when at home he walked in the fields or woods, and returned to write down in his study his thoughts or observations. These he would work over until they suited him, and then, following the custom of that day when so much of America's thinking was expressed from the lecture platform, he would set forth on his tours, delivering in towns and cities the lectures which he later published as his essays.

Emerson's one systematic book is *Nature,* his earliest. It has structural form; the thought can be outlined from beginning to end. The book was published in 1836. But no other was so written according to plan. The remainder of his many volumes contain his essays, each written to a title and around a central subject which it illumines rather than dissects. The reader does not finish one and rise with the complete knowledge of Emerson's thought upon it, whether it be "History," "Self-Reliance," "Spiritual Laws," "Prudence," "Heroism," or "Friendship" (to take some of the titles in the First Series of his *Essays*). Instead the reader rises inspired with thoughts aroused by the essay, and with his own conduct attuned to following them. Few essays did more to strengthen the young men of the day than the second of these, "Self-Reliance," with the ancient injunction, "Know Thyself," fortified by the advice, "Trust Thyself."

The lecture system of those days was aided by the innumerable lyceums which, originating in New England, spread all over the country to towns of any size. In the lyceums, forerunners of the Chautauqua, Emerson lectured for many years, meeting the hardships naturally inherent in the stagecoaches, the crude sleeping cars, the badly heated hotels of mid-nineteenth-century America. Famous from his beginning, yet under suspicion because of his almost revolutionary thought, he made his way to complete acceptance, until his words were household in all forward-looking families in a period of controversy when new ideas were resisted by the old, welcomed by the young. Emerson was the prophet of youth when in the spiritual war against slavery the nation was coming to take sides, when the radicalism of intellectual Europe was assuming its own form on American shores, and when the old theology was crumbling, partly under his blows.

He first shocked the Puritan world, long entrenched, self-satisfied, and crystallized into a dead formalism, by his Harvard Divinity School Address in 1838. Men of the old school at once protested at thoughts disturbingly new; it was many years before that center of conservatism invited him again. Yet invited again he was, after a long battle in which the odds turned to his side. Emerson welcomed the new science, so disturbing to the old theology. He advocated new social ideas, now fundamental and instinctive with all America. His method was not to attack the old, but to state the new, and let his ideas stand or fall by themselves, without defense or rejoinder by him. And so sure was he of his ground, so telling in the simple force of his principles, that opponents were silenced, and support grew. Long before his death he was the venerated prophet of the new America.

One does not dissect and explain Emerson's philosophy as one can explain the structure of some other system of thought. For Emerson's ideas can never be so formulated: they are rather a way of life, never dry, always inspiring thought and action.

Some of his most memorable writing is in his poems, which cover a wide range of technical performance, more usually a vehicle for the bare simplicity of his thought than for beauty of phrase. Therefore they are sometimes more rugged than easy, more difficult than comprehensible. Yet Emerson occupies a secure place as an American poet; and his range is wide, from the childlike humor of "The Mountain and the Squirrel," through the pure beauty of "The Rhodora," to the cryptic obscurity of his "Brahma." In the latter appears a nugget of what is called Emerson's Transcendentalism, the uplifting thought that over us all is a spirit which will strengthen and lead us. This is given more concisely still in the two lines upon his tombstone, which express the spiritual aim of Emerson's whole life and achievement: "The passive master lent his hand / To the vast soul which o'er him planned."

A proof of the depth of Emerson's wisdom was that he allied himself with but one of the new movements of his day. America was full of enthusiasts and prophets, mystics, founders of experiments in social living. They flocked to Emerson's door; he saw the weaknesses of their ideas, yet he was very patient with them. He would not join with them, however. He did not go to Brook Farm, as Hawthorne did; nor would he take part in Alcott's Fruitlands. He went his way alone, except that upon due deliberation he supported the growing abolitionism. Yet he would not share its extremes nor its violence. He gave to it his ideas, and they gradually made their way.

Conservative Concord, though from the first it respected Emerson, was slow in following him. Said one prominent citizen to him, early in the slavery controversy, "There are only three persons, as far as I know, whose opinions are obnoxious to the members of our community: they are, Theodore Parker, Wendell Phillips, and—if I may be so candid—yourself,

Ralph Waldo Emerson, 1860s, from cabinet card by J. W. Black

Sir." But Concord eventually followed and supported him. And personally he was always respected and beloved. The town knew him in all his transparent ways, whether working in his garden; or walking in the streets and fields and woods; or sitting in silence at town meetings, where he admired the rugged eloquence of the speakers; or beating down with his cane a sign insulting the town doctor, advocate of temperance, which drinkers had hung upon the Mill Dam. Emerson had no concealments, no politics, no hesitation to speak his mind, no superiority to the simpler people around him. He was no crank, no unbalanced reformer. Gentle in manner, plain in dress, unaffected in all his ways, a true neighbor, he was yet known to be inflexible in principle and fearless of all entrenched conservatism that opposed (but so vainly) the innovations of his thought.

Emerson's life in Concord was that of a plain citizen, claiming nothing from his acknowledged eminence. He was never aloof, as was Hawthorne in his way, or Thoreau in his. Emerson served on committees. He had a strange regret for the scholarliness which he could not put off, and which barred him from the impromptu forum of the blacksmith shop or the street corner. His townsmen he always respected, and he envied practical ability wherever he saw it. Wrote he: "I like people who can do things. When Edward and I struggled in vain to drag our big calf into the barn, the Irish girl put her finger in the calf's mouth and led her in directly." By the same token Emerson was a poor gardener and clumsy with tools. His little boy said to him, "Papa, I'm afraid you'll dig your leg." A committee of the Horticultural Society called upon him to see the soil which produced such poor specimens of such fine varieties. Emerson was amused at his own limitations, admitted them, and perceived their warning. "I stoop to pull up a weed that is choking the corn, and find there are two; close behind is a third; behind that there are four thousand and one. I am heated and untuned." He concluded, "The scholar shall not dig."

But if gardening tired him and unfitted him for the study, walking did not. Though slender and apparently frail, he was a tireless walker, and found in the woods and fields stimulus for thought. The farmers knew that he respected them; on their ground he was a learner.

On the other hand, when he spoke to them from the lyceum platform he gave them his best, never speaking down to them. One farmer claimed to have heard all of Mr. Emerson's lectures, and added, "And understood 'em too." A Concord workwoman, helping at Madam Hoar's, went home early one afternoon: she was going to Mr. Emerson's lecture. Asked if she understood him, she answered, "Not a word, but I like to go and see him stand up there and look as if he thought everyone was as good as he was."

The only unkind action toward Emerson in his town was effectually checked. A neighbor sought to blackmail him by moving an ugly old shed into the lot before his house. In the night a number of young men, provided with ropes, hooks, and a ladder, came and pulled the old thing down. They were never named; but Emerson's son, writing of this many years afterward, implied that it was perfectly known who they were.

And when his house caught fire, never was neighborly help more complete in saving books, papers, and furniture, and in putting out the fire. The excitement and exposure of the incident threatened Emerson's health; but his neighbors and friends combined to send him abroad and repair the building. He went to Europe and Egypt with his daughter, recruited his strength, and when he returned was welcomed by his townspeople, who led him, under a triumphal arch, to the restored house. At first believing that the welcome was to his daughter, at last he perceived its meaning, and going back to the gate, said to them all, "My friends, I know that this is not a tribute to an old man and his daughter returned to their house, but to the common blood of us—all one family—in Concord!"

Emerson died, enfeebled by age, in 1882, and was buried in Sleepy Hollow Cemetery, where others of his name lie around him.

Bronson Alcott

It was in 1840 that Amos Bronson Alcott, drawn by his friendship with Emerson, came to Concord and lived in the Hosmer Cottage far out on Main Street. Here soon afterward was born the last of his four daughters. Alcott, born in Connecticut in 1799, once a peddler and tutor in the South, and but lately the owner of the unsuccessful Temple School in Boston, was a reformer in education, a writer whose first book remained largely unsold, and a philosopher whose *Conversations with Children on the Gospels* had brought him something of fame but little in money. So poor was he and unpretentious in his ways that he began in Concord, besides tilling his own garden, as a day laborer in the fields. In the winter that followed he chopped wood in Concord woodlots for a dollar a day. As he grew poorer, he did much of the housework; and from clothes handed down to his daughters he designed and cut dresses for them. But in 1842, on Emerson's money, he went to England to see unknown friends who admired him through his writings, and returned bringing the Englishman Charles Lane, and the idea of setting up a new venture in living, philosophical, vegetarian—and sadly impractical. It was begun at Fruitlands in the town of Harvard in 1843, and after but a single season came to complete failure. Alcott's disappointment and disillusion were so great that he wished to die; but nature was too strong. In 1844, again with Emerson's help, he returned to Concord, and the next year moved into the house on Lexington Road which he called Hillside, later to become Hawthorne's Wayside. By planting and hard labor he improved the place within and without, and lived there several years.

Emerson wrote of Alcott, "He is a great man . . . His conversation is sublime . . . Yet when I see how he is underestimated by cultivated people, I fancy none but I have heard him talk." But perhaps Emerson gave Alcott an inspiration that no one else could supply. At any rate, Concord, and the wider world of his day, never understood Alcott—and he took a deal of understanding. He never learned the value of money, and his wife and children carried many cares of which he seemed unaware. Unpractical, though a hard worker with his hands, according to all worldly standards he was improvident, depending as he did upon the guidance of one higher than himself. His books brought him little money; his lecture tours brought him almost less, for from one he returned with but a dollar in cash. The help of Emerson tided him through his worst period. Yet the Sage of Concord

Amos Bronson Alcott in Orchard House study, 1870s, from card stereograph

was serene and untroubled among difficulties which he hardly perceived. His trust in Providence was sublime: once it all but confounded his loving but doubting family. On a snowy winter's night, when characteristically the supply of wood was very low, a neighbor's child came and begged fuel, for there was a baby in the house, and no money. Mrs. Alcott hesitated: she also had a baby. But Alcott said, "Give half our stock. The weather will moderate, or wood will come." The wood was given, but the weather grew worse, and at bedtime the Alcotts were about to cover their fire to keep it, when a farmer knocked at the door. He had started for Boston with a load of wood, but the drifts were so bad that he asked if he might not drop the wood in the Alcott's yard. Alcott might pay for it at any time. The family was deeply impressed; the incident seemed to justify one of Mrs. Alcott's sayings: "Cast your bread upon the waters, and after many days it will come back buttered."

With providential and with neighborly care Alcott plodded on. A certain amount of recognition came to him, very comforting when Concord, recognizing at last the worth of his educational ideas, made him superintendent of its schools. But he was always idealistic and impractical, as his daughter once humorously indicated. He had at length set up in Concord his longed-for School of Philosophy, which in its short life caused a pleasant flutter among the many theorists of the day. Miss Alcott, being asked to define a philosopher, said that he was a man up in a balloon, with his family holding to the ropes and trying to haul him back to earth.

Fortunately this very daughter Louisa held the strongest rope. She never hauled him down; but she sent up ample supplies, so that he and his fellow dreamers could hover above the earth in comfort. Her story is one of real heroism.

Louisa Alcott

Louisa May Alcott was in 1832 born into this family where everything revolved around the father, and where hardship was cheerfully borne because of the ideals which he taught and lived up to. He was almost her only teacher; but he wisely encouraged on the one hand the romping which made her strong in youth, and on the other the play of fancy by which she came to live. Her attitude toward him was tenderly protective. For need of money she helped out at home and tried domestic service; but from first to last she stuck to her writing. She had some small success with the magazines. She went to the Civil War as a nurse, caught typhoid pneumonia, and though she survived it, it was at the cost of her health. She said that she had never been ill before, and never well afterward.

But with inborn courage and persistence, she continued her work. A publisher advised her to teach; but she answered that she would not—she would prove that she could write.

Her *Hospital Sketches* of her Civil War experiences had some success; but *Moods*, her first novel, was not profitable. Then another publisher asked her to write a girls' book. She answered, "I'll try." The result was *Little Women*.

The success of this book made her reputation and the family fortune. Other books followed, very popular in their day, and still read in ours. Yet they are, almost without exception, juvenile fiction. Only *Little Women* reaches up to the full stature of a novel. Its portrayal of the humors of the childhood of the Alcott sisters, their difficulties and struggles on reaching maturity, the tragedy of a death, and the romance of three marriages, has pleased and touched generations of readers. No book written in Concord (it was, however, but partly written in the Orchard House) has had such a vogue or such financial success. The Alcott family burden was lifted. The father took it placidly, as he took everything. And Louisa continued writing.

The story of Louisa Alcott is, therefore, one of dogged courage triumphant over difficulties. Not great as a stylist or a thinker, she knew how to reach the heart. Few have more deserved success. It should be better known that she wrote two touching poems: one on Thoreau's death ("Thoreau's Flute") and one to her aged and helpless father. He died on the fourth of March 1888, she but two days later. Both lie buried in Sleepy Hollow.

The oldest sister, Anna, married and lived in Concord. A measure of artistic success and fame came to the youngest, May. She was the first teacher of Daniel Chester French, the sculptor, and in her own right a good painter, though best known for her copies of Turner. She married and lived abroad; but her youthful drawings on the walls of Orchard House are well known to tourists.

Louisa May Alcott, 1880s, from cabinet card by J. Notman

Thoreau

Another Concord writer, competing in fame with Emerson, is Henry David Thoreau. His still growing reputation amounts, with some students, almost to a cult. He was a prophet of individualism, a student of nature, a writer whose method of life and subject matter set him apart from all others. The comparison of him with Emerson is inevitable: their habits of work were the same, in producing books culled from voluminous journals. Alcott did the like, to be sure; but his books are pale and spineless compared with Emerson's, and even Emerson's lack the vigor of Thoreau. In the latter's essays he touches upon Emerson's ground, not always to his own advantage. But Thoreau was no imitator, except in his early unconscious following of more mature thought. Least of all did he imitate anyone in his particular field of writing or in his way of life.

Of this last it has been humorously said that it is popularly believed that Thoreau spent half of his life in Concord Jail and half in Walden Woods. The germ of truth in this is that he spent practically all of his life in Concord. His travels were brief; his longest stay was a year spent in tutoring on Staten Island, from which he was glad to return. But he said of himself, "I have travelled a good deal in Concord." And though his neighbors considered him idle, the reality is a life of steady purpose in developing his own genius. This was as peculiar as that of any American writer, yet resulted in a permanent source of inspiration to many since his day.

Henry David Thoreau, 1861, from cabinet card reproduction of original ambrotype by E. S. Dunshee

Thoreau was born in 1817 in a house on the Virginia Road; he was christened David Henry, a sequence which he later reversed. He went to school in Concord and to college at Harvard, and began life as teacher in the Concord public school. But

Deacon Nehemiah Ball objected to the absence of whipping, whereupon Thoreau whipped half a dozen pupils in one afternoon and then resigned as a teacher. He then set up a school with his brother John, to whom he was devoted. But John died suddenly of lockjaw, a terrible blow to Henry. He lived then for awhile in the Emerson household, in which at other periods he was a member of the family. Clever with his hands as few others were, he was useful about the place, practical helper in all household matters, and companion and friend to the children.

In 1845, following a plan which he had long had in his mind, Thoreau built himself a hut on Emerson's land on Walden Pond, lived there for a little more than two years.[11] His time he spent wandering in the woods, writing in his journal, and completing the manuscript of his *Week on the Concord and Merrimack Rivers*, the half-philosophic journal of a trip taken some years earlier with his brother. Finding no publisher, he brought out the work at his own expense, and later had to store at home in the village the unsold copies. He now had a library, he said, of a thousand volumes, over seven hundred of which he had written himself. It was not until 1854 that he brought out *Walden*, a book arising from his experiences at the pond, and on which, to most people, his fame rests. It is a very personal and direct account of his life there, with a semi-narrative quality impossible to Emerson. It is in fact the personal quality of his work that gives Thoreau's writings their force and interest, while Emerson's personality lies hidden.

There is, however, one more quality to the book (and to the best of Thoreau's writings) which gives it its timelessness. That is its social gospel—the need of each soul to depend upon itself, and to break free of the shackles of human conventions and ancient institutions. This scorn of what others accepted is more prominent still in his "Plea for Captain John Brown" and his "Civil Disobedience," the latter said to have been in great part the inspiration of Ghandi.

Besides these two books and a few essays and speeches, Thoreau printed nothing in his lifetime. Much was published after his death, however, including many of his journals. Necessary to his life at home, after Walden, were his wide wanderings in the town and in fact in the region. If he wanted to go anywhere he would strike across country afoot. His costume was unconventional, his manners abrupt; to strangers he was crusty, and even to his friends he was "with difficulty, sweet." Yet he had a few close friends, the poet Channing, Emerson himself, Alcott, and others less known. In his own fashion he let people see how little he cared for their ways. In protest against the Mexican War he refused to pay his poll tax, and therefore was put in jail. But the stay was for a single night, as his aunt paid the tax, and he was set free.[12]

Thoreau never married. His youthful love affair with Ellen Sewall (who refused both brothers) was short and on his part Transcendentally lofty. She cannot have understood him, and he was not easy to understand. Disappointed though he may have been, he had no self-pity. And viewed at this distance, a married Thoreau seems impossible. If for a time the dream seemed to lure him from his course, the vision faded. The experience threw him still further back into himself, and he went his strange way, free of all such ties.

Thoreau was mistaken in his claim that he was independent of society, that he lived on the few beans that he raised at Walden, or on the few dollars that later he chose to earn yearly. He squatted on Emerson's land; before and afterward he lived with his parents and sisters. Money for his personal needs he earned by lecturing (at which he never was a success), by surveying or by carpentering, or in his father's pencil factory. It is not true that when he had learned to make a perfect pencil he gave up making more; the truth was that his improved method of making graphite was more profitable and drove the other business out. Nevertheless, while Thoreau was more dependent on society at large than he cared to acknowledge, in all his ways he was aloof. He simplified his life. In Concord affairs he took no part except when he lectured at the lyceum, or when in his indignation at the fate of John Brown he called the town together to listen to his "Plea." A timorous friend advised him to give up the plan. He replied that there was to be a meeting, and that he would speak. His courage, in large ways like this when public opinion was against him, or in the small ways of manners and daily life, was not to be questioned. The force of his example and the power of his words have inspired many to follow him in breaking free from the minor absurdities of custom or the great injustices of a complacent society. And in these ways he is still a force.

Perhaps the intensity with which he lived his life, thought his thoughts, and expressed them in his striking fashion wore down the oaken strength which Emerson admired. He was reckless of exposure, and a cold gave way to consumption. As he lay dying in his Main Street house, a relative ventured to ask him if he had made his peace with God. The independent, free in religion as in everything else, replied, "I didn't know that we had ever quarrelled, Aunt." He died in 1862, and, like the others of whom we have written here, lies on the ridge in Sleepy Hollow.

Hawthorne

Nathaniel Hawthorne, more of an outsider than all the rest, more solitary in Concord streets than Thoreau at Walden, is yet more identified with Concord than with any other of his various residences. Born in Salem in 1804, he lived in his youth the life of a recluse even in his own home, and emerged only gradually into the outer world. Always a writer, but without marked early success, he spent a year at the idealistic Brook Farm. Then marrying, he brought his bride to Concord in 1842, to live three years in the house which, following the title he gave the book that he wrote there, *Mosses from an Old Manse,* has ever since been called the Old Manse. But the book failed to remove the pressure of necessity; for the needs of his family he accepted an appointment at the Salem Customs House, and so in 1845 brought to an end his first Concord period.

In spite of the need of money, however, his life in the Manse was idyllic. Thoroughly happy in his wife, he desired no other human companionship, would sometimes flee when strangers appeared, and once when his wife was away for two days he took pride in speaking to no one, not even the servant. He worked in his garden before the house, and often was seen standing long periods in meditation, leaning upon his hoe. He walked to the village for his mail, shy of all that he met. And he wandered in the fields, or rowed on the river in the boat which he bought from Thoreau, sometimes with Thoreau himself.

For he was ready to receive certain friends who had secured his approval. Emerson would come, and Channing the poet, and Thoreau, whose silence was like Hawthorne's own. Margaret Fuller was an occasional visitor. Also there came friends from other places, such as Franklin Pierce, not yet president. Hawthorne was constant in his affections, though closest of all to his heart was his love for his wife and children.

In 1852 Hawthorne returned again to Concord. His novels *The Scarlet Letter, The House of the Seven Gables* and *The Blithedale Romance* had brought him success. In the *Romance*, the scene of the searching for the body of the drowned Zenobia was drawn from an incident in Concord itself. More prosperous now, Hawthorne bought Alcott's Hillside, named it Wayside, and fitted it for his occupancy. Here he collected some of his earlier stories, and wrote *Tanglewood Tales*. Here also, at the request of Franklin Pierce, then campaigning for the presidency, he wrote for him a campaign biography.

Although no longer so great a recluse, Hawthorne was still shy. He spent long hours meditating on the ridge behind his house, and when descending, Alcott said, "if he caught sight of any one in the road he would go under cover like a partridge." He knew the town so little that when the Emerson children showed him pictures of the Square and the Mill Dam he asked where they were.

When Pierce was elected president he offered Hawthorne the consulship at Liverpool. After but a year at Concord, therefore, Hawthorne went away again, to stay abroad seven years. He traveled on the continent, made with his *Marble Faun* still more success, and returned in 1860 almost a man of the world. In company he now met people readily; yet he would withdraw himself, to meditate on the problems which burdened him. The charge that he was gloomy, at least in the subjects of his stories, was always denied by his worshiping wife. He was, she said, "like a stray Seraph, who had experienced in his life no evil, but . . . saw and sorrowed over evil."

If we accept that explanation, his vision and his sorrow overcame him in the last few years of his life. The Civil War oppressed him, some physical cause also may have sapped his strength, and he could do no

Nathaniel Hawthorne, 1860, from carte de visite by J. J. E. Mayall

steady work. In the tower which he built on top of Wayside, where he could be safe from interruption, or in meditating long upon his ridge, he could not bring to a satisfactory end the four separate novels which he tried to write. His mysterious burdens were too great. At length, going away with Pierce for a vacation in New Hampshire, he died in his sleep on the night of the eighteenth-nineteenth of May 1864. His body was brought back to Concord and he lies buried near his famous friends.

Emerson, the Alcotts, Thoreau, and Hawthorne are the group on whom the literary fame of Concord will most securely rest. Other well-known writers have lived in Concord for longer or shorter periods, notably Margaret Fuller, George William Curtis, the younger William Ellery Channing (the poet), Franklin B. Sanborn, and Jane Austin, the American historical novelist. Here lived also Mrs. Daniel Lothrop (Margaret Sidney), author of the "Five Little Peppers" books. But these are either less in fame or of a later time. We stop, chronologically, with the death of the Alcotts, and leave to a later or a larger book the many facts and anecdotes about those who, in this or other fields of endeavor, have added to the reputation of Concord.

NOTES TO HISTORY

1. Allen French here refers to Clamshell Hill, a Native American midden on the Sudbury River and a source of artifacts for later collectors, among them Henry David Thoreau. The remains of Clamshell Hill were razed for Emerson Hospital parking in the 1960s, well after French wrote these words.—*LPW*

2. The word "savages" is, of course, now considered disrespectful. If he were writing today, French would no doubt have preferred another term.—*LPW*

3. The rivers are the Sudbury and the Assabet, which at Egg Rock meet and form the Concord, which empties into the Merrimack. Though never useful for navigation, they were formerly a great means of recreation, as proved by George Bartlett's guidebook of 1880; he addressed his book, not merely to Concord pleasure seekers, but also to tourists coming by water from farther away.—*AF*

4. The original grant for Concord consisted of a six-mile square, which, as Ruth Robinson Wheeler noted in her *Concord: Climate for Freedom*, "established a standard size for towns in later grants throughout Massachusetts" (page 13). Later, Concord's geographic area shrank as parts of it broke off to form independent towns (Bedford, Acton, Lincoln, and Carlisle).—*LPW*

5. Lexington historian Richard Kollen comments that Allen French here overstates the influence of Adams and Hancock in the Provincial Congress, the leadership of which reflected the range of interests of participants from across Massachusetts. Also, in response to the chronology of events presented by French two paragraphs later, Kollen points out that the first muster of the militia on the Green took place after the arrival first of Revere, then Dawes.—*LPW*

6. Strictly speaking, Lexington had a militia company, but no minute men. When Allen French referred to the Revolutionary soldiers of Lexington as "minute men," he followed a common practice of his time. He clearly understood the difference between Colonial minute and militia companies, as is shown in the first few paragraphs of his "The Revolutionary Period" section of *Historic Concord*. However, in writing about Lexington specifically, he seems to have deferred to that town's own loose use of the term "minute men" in the first half of the twentieth century (revealed, for example, on more than one Revolutionary monument there). Later historians of the Lexington Fight (David Hackett Fischer in his *Paul Revere's Ride*, for instance) have been more careful in observing the distinction.—*LPW*

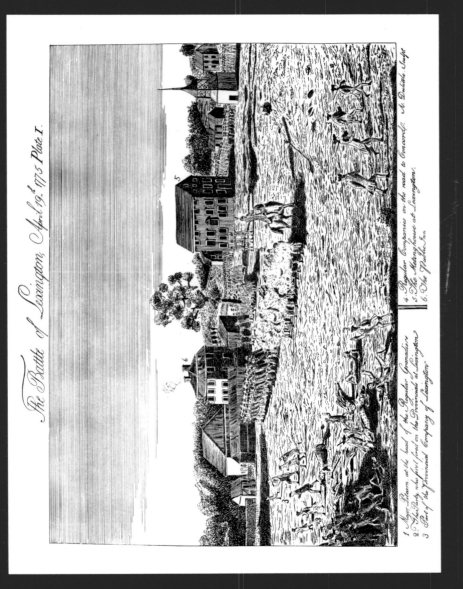

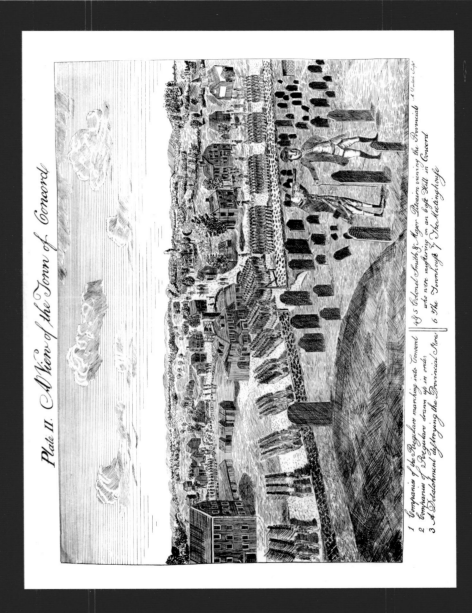

PLATE I *The Battle of Lexington,* 1775,
from engraving by Amos Doolittle

PLATE II *A View of the Town of Concord,* 1775,
from engraving by Amos Doolittle

Map of
Historic Concord
As It Is Today

1/2 mile

To Carlisle

To Estabrook Woods

Spencer Brook

Barrett's Mill

Barrett Farm

Hildreth House

Barrett's Mill Road

Hildreth's Corner

Assabet River

Minute Man National Historical Park

Buttrick House

Street

Concord River

Great Meadows National Wildlife Refuge

Monsen Road

Old Bedford Road

Musterfield

North Bridge Visitor's Center

Old North Bridge
Battle Monument

The Robbins House

P

Lowell Road

Liberty Street

Minute Man Statue

Hunt-Hosmer House

Hunt's Bridge

Grave of the British Soldiers

Old Manse

Elisha Jones House

Virginia Road

To Thoreau's Birthplace

N
W   E
S

Old Calf Pasture

Egg Rock

Monument Street

Sleepy Hollow Cemetery

62

Bedford Street

Nashawtuc Hill

Peter Bulkeley marker

Meriam House

Elm Street

Sanborn House

South Burying Ground

Keyes Road

Pellet-Barrett House

Art Association/Ball House

Reuben Brown House

Heywood Meadow & Gun House

The Wayside

Orchard House

Grapevine Cottage

Old Bedford Road

Meriam's Corner

South Bridge Boat House

Thoreau-Alcott House

Main Street

Concord Free Public Library

P

P

Concord Museum

Emerson House

P

Lexington Road

Minute Man National Historical Park

To West Concord

Dovecote

Joseph Hosmer House

South Bridge

Concord Depot

Sudbury Road

Thoreau Street

Walden Street

Mill Brook

Main Street

62

2

Sudbury River

Monument Square

The Cottage

Colonial Inn

Spanish-American War Memorial

Masonic Temple

Holy Family Rectory

County Jail Site

Mill Brook

P

Visitor's Center

Veterans' Memorial & Middlesex Hotel Site

Main Street

Soldiers' Monument

World War I Memorial

Flagpole

Grave of the Third British Soldier

Concord Courthouse

Town House

Dee Funeral Home

Holy Family Church

Hill Burying Ground

Wright Tavern

First Parish Church

Cambridge Turnpike

2A

To Lexington

2

To Nine Acre Corner

P = Parking

To Thoreau's Cabin Site

126

Walden Pond

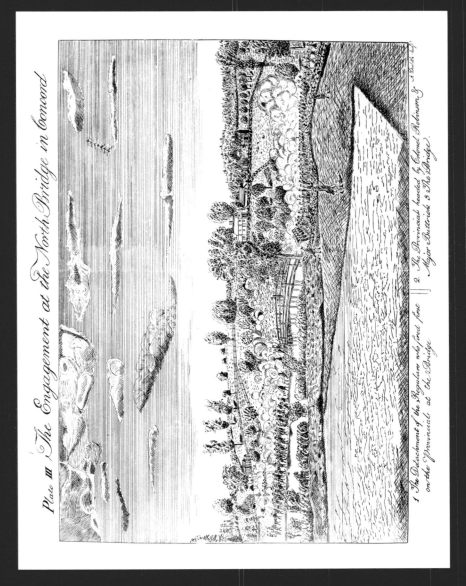

PLATE III *The Engagement at the North Bridge in Concord*, 1775,
from engraving by Amos Doolittle

PLATE IV *A View of the South part of Lexington*, 1775,
from engraving by Amos Doolittle

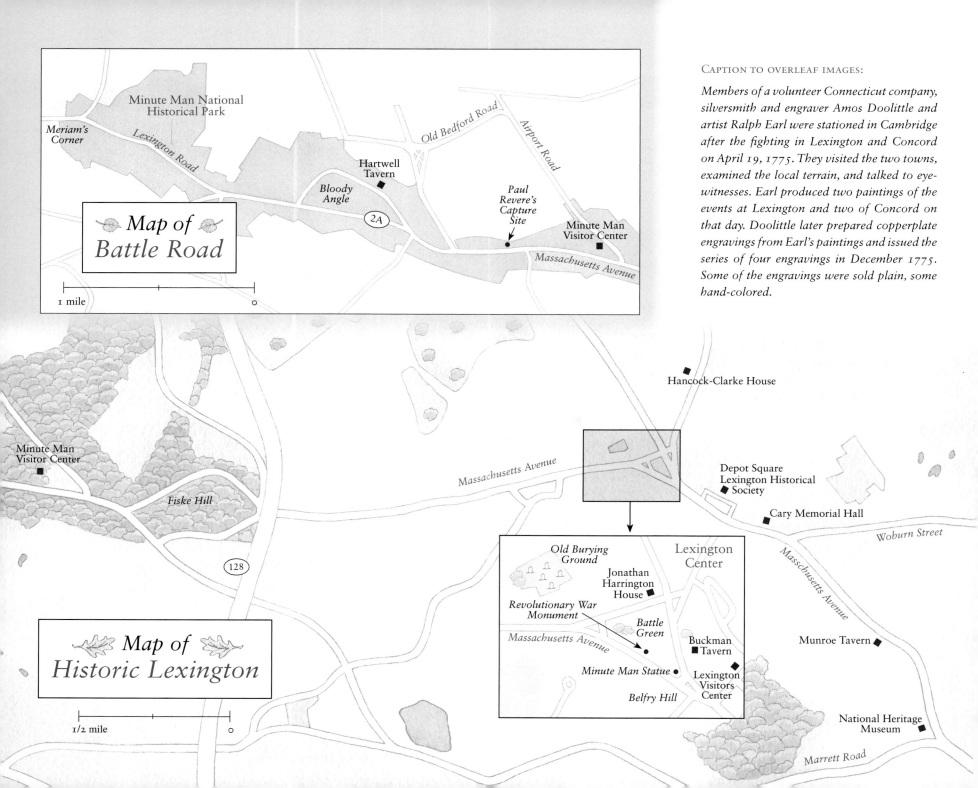

Map of Battle Road

Minute Man National Historical Park

Meriam's Corner

Lexington Road

Old Bedford Road

Airport Road

Hartwell Tavern

Bloody Angle

2A

Paul Revere's Capture Site

Minute Man Visitor Center

Massachusetts Avenue

1 mile

CAPTION TO OVERLEAF IMAGES:

Members of a volunteer Connecticut company, silversmith and engraver Amos Doolittle and artist Ralph Earl were stationed in Cambridge after the fighting in Lexington and Concord on April 19, 1775. They visited the two towns, examined the local terrain, and talked to eye-witnesses. Earl produced two paintings of the events at Lexington and two of Concord on that day. Doolittle later prepared copperplate engravings from Earl's paintings and issued the series of four engravings in December 1775. Some of the engravings were sold plain, some hand-colored.

Map of Historic Lexington

Minute Man Visitor Center

Fiske Hill

128

Massachusetts Avenue

Hancock-Clarke House

Depot Square Lexington Historical Society

Cary Memorial Hall

Woburn Street

Massachusetts Avenue

Munroe Tavern

National Heritage Museum

Marrett Road

1/2 mile

Lexington Center

Old Burying Ground

Jonathan Harrington House

Revolutionary War Monument

Battle Green

Massachusetts Avenue

Buckman Tavern

Minute Man Statue

Lexington Visitors Center

Belfry Hill

7. The Colonial soldiers of April 19, 1775, can be called "Americans" only retrospectively.—*LPW*

8. Richard Kollen suggests that Parker would have been more likely to speak these words when facing the regulars on the Green—not as they approached. He also notes that there is conflicting evidence about the Jonathan Harrington story told several paragraphs down.—*LPW*

9. Ephraim Jones's tavern was located in the vicinity of the South, or Main Street, Burying Ground, near which stood Concord's jail during the Revolution.—*LPW*

10. A gunflint (the flint of a flintlock, used to strike fire, the only method of those days) was square, entirely different from an Indian arrowhead. Flint of this quality is not native stone.—*AF*

11. The exact location of Thoreau's house at Walden Pond has long been a matter of controversy. It was moved away and the chimney taken down shortly after he vacated it. The cairn erected by admirers on its supposed site was not begun until 1872, when all traces of the building had disappeared. Depending on the memory of friends, a spot was chosen as the probable position of the hut. But, since it did not tally with Thoreau's minute description of it in *Walden,* it has always raised questions. Other spots have been pointed out as more probable, and even marked with corner-posts, but not until 1945 did anyone have the curiosity and perseverance to solve the problem.

    Roland Wells Robbins of Lincoln, Massachusetts, had the practical idea of searching the sandy hillside for the foundation *of the chimney.* After many weeks of probing and digging he finally unearthed the unmistakable evidence he needed. In his book *Discovery at Walden,* he tells step by step the fascinating story. The hearth had been removed and the accumulation of a century had obscured the traces on the surface, but the solid masonry of the foundations was exposed, untouched since Thoreau built it with his own hands. Later, three corner-posts and a center-post of the house and four corners of the woodshed were found, as well as many other proofs which are incontrovertible.

    The exact shape and position of the house being now settled, it is expected that a suitable marker will be placed on the hearth. It is interesting to note Mr. Robbins' discovery places the house in the exact location shown on Thoreau's own map!—*AF*

12. Accounts vary as to who paid Thoreau's tax.—*LPW*

AF = Allen French
LPW = Leslie Perrin Wilson

GUIDE

*to Concord
and to Sites
Associated
with the
Lexington Fight*

BY LESLIE PERRIN WILSON

*Concord Free
Public Library,
1870s, detail
from cabinet card*

CONCORD GUIDE

Minute Man Visitor Center

The Minute Man Visitor Center of the Minute Man National Historical Park is a useful first stop for sightseers headed by car to either Concord or Lexington. Located on Route 2A in Lexington (at the Lexington/Lincoln line), this facility is about half a mile west of Route I-95/128 (watch for signage for the exit to Route 2A West). Maps, brochures, and guides to local sites, a gift shop and bookstore, and public restrooms are all available here. There is an impressive forty-foot mural depicting the conflict between British and Colonial soldiers on April 19, 1775, and a theater in which a twenty-minute orientation film ("The Road to Revolution") is shown at half-hour intervals. Accessible from the Visitor Center, the Battle Road Trail accommodates walking and bicycling through fields, wetlands, and woods, past stone walls (original and recreated), archaeological sites, and restored Colonial buildings. The Minute Man Visitor Center is open April through October. For more information about the Minute Man National Historical Park, visit the Web pages at http://www.nps.gov/mima, or contact park headquarters at (978) 369-6993.

To reach downtown Concord from the Minute Man Visitor Center, continue west on 2A, taking a right where Lexington Road turns off from 2A, and follow it all the way into Monument Square.

Concord Visitor Center

Reflecting Concord's layered history and sitting at a major confluence of roads, Monument Square is a natural starting point for the visitor. But before mapping out a prospective itinerary from the Square, the sightseer will want to stop at the nearby Concord Visitor Center, located at 58 Main Street (one block west of Monument Square), in the heart of the Concord Center business district, behind the Middlesex Savings Bank at the corner of Main Street and Keyes Road.

To reach Concord from Boston and Cambridge, the traveler should head west on Route 2 as far as Exit 50 at the foot of the hill on

the Concord/Lincoln boundary. Route 2 veers sharply left at that point
(Crosby's Corner), but the visitor should stay in the far right lane and
go straight across the highway onto the Cambridge Turnpike, following it for about a mile to its intersection with Lexington Road. (The
Concord Museum is situated to the right just before the intersection,
the Emerson House to the left.) Making a left turn onto Lexington
Road, the traveler quickly reaches Monument Square, identifiable by
the Wright Tavern to the left, a traffic rotary with flagpole, and the
Civil War obelisk on the Common. To reach the Visitor Center, go
to the left around the rotary to Main Street (which lies roughly at a
right angle with Lexington Road). The first street on the right is Keyes
Road, taking which the visitor will find public parking on the right,
directly behind the bank.

Built with combined public and private funding and dedicated in
2002, the Visitor Center on Main Street replaced a very modest facility
on Heywood Street. Operated by the Concord Chamber of Commerce, the new facility is open regular hours daily from spring into
fall. The Visitor Center provides maps, brochures, and other useful literature; the assistance of trained personnel; a variety of Concord-related books and products for purchase; regularly-scheduled,
seasonally-available guided walking tours and by-appointment group
or individual tours; and handicapped-accessible public restrooms
open year-round from 7:00 A.M. to 8:00 P.M. (See http://www.concord
chamberofcommerce.org/visitor-information/ for details.)

Setting Out from Monument Square

Tours of Concord—guided and self-guided—often begin at the end of
Monument Square by the Colonial Inn (across the Common as approached from Lexington Road), where buses and trolleys drop off
visitors to explore historic sites, to shop, or to find a place to eat. (The
Liberty Ride trolley out of Lexington—a project of the Town of Lexington's Tourism Committee—stops here, as well as on Keyes Road,
near the Concord Visitor Center; see http://www.libertyride.us/liberty-
ride.html for more information.)

Five important Concord roads come together in Monument
Square. As the visitor stands directly in front of and facing the

Colonial Inn, Lowell Road runs out of the Square to the left,
Monument Street to the right. With back to the Inn, the visitor faces
the Common and observes Main Street running off to the right (into
Concord's business district) and Bedford Street to the left (between
the Town House and the Holy Family Church) at the opposite end of
the Common. Beyond the Common, a traffic rotary circles a second,
smaller grassed area, where stands the flagpole. Beyond the rotary,
Lexington Road heads east.

Starting out in Monument Square, the tourist unconstrained by
time might take in most of the major local historical and literary sites
by systematically following these five roads. These roads also provide
a framework for planning the selective itineraries of those who must
choose what they most want to see in Concord.

*Monument Square, showing Town House, Catholic church, and flagpole,
ca. 1895, by Alfred Munroe*

Monument Square

From the seventeenth century, Monument Square has been central to Concord's civic, recreational, religious, educational, commercial, military, and ceremonial life. The formal purchase of land by English settlers from the local Native Americans took place on August 5, 1637, on the north side of Main Street as it runs off the Square, under an oak later dubbed "Jethro's Tree." Peter Bulkeley—a founder and the first minister of Concord—held significant property and lived on what is now known as the Square. Military training took place on a field that formed part of the Common. The town's early church (its only church until the nineteenth century) sat on the outskirts of the Square, originally on the hill on the side of the present Lexington Road across from where the First Parish Church stands today. Concord's first cemetery was located on this same hill. Later, when there was some denominational choice, other churches were built on the Square.

Because Concord was a seat of the Middlesex County courts from the seventeenth century into the nineteenth, the church building at first doubled as a courthouse. It also accommodated town meeting, that traditional New England form of government at which local citizens—both the high-born and the humble—debate and vote on local issues.

Later, a hotel and bar serving those with business in Concord stood on the Square, as did general stores to supply the needs and wants of Concord people, and also the public schoolhouse where Henry David Thoreau briefly taught following his graduation from Harvard College. Concord's rich nineteenth-century intellectual life was nourished here, as Ralph Waldo Emerson, Henry David Thoreau, and other local lights spoke before gatherings of the Concord Lyceum, which from mid-century met regularly in the Town House.

On April 19, 1689, Concord's militia company marched from the Square to Boston to assist in deposing Governor Andros. On April 19, 1775, British troops made their headquarters in the Wright Tavern (located at the head of Main Street, across from where Jethro's Tree once stood). After the Concord Fight, one of the British soldiers who died as a result of wounds sustained at the North Bridge was buried at the corner where the Square meets Monument Street. In September 1786, during the rebellion led in Massachusetts by Daniel Shays, Job

Shattuck of Groton and a crowd of rioters occupied the Square and obstructed the courts to protest widespread economic hardship and inequity. And on April 19, 1861, the Concord Artillery Company left from here for Civil War service.

The historical significance of the Square was recognized in the creation of the Monument Square-Lexington Road Historic District. But Monument Square hardly presents a static historic façade. It is still central to Concord town life. Residents of the town pay bills and transact other municipal business daily in the Town House, attend church services, take in lectures, observe holidays and celebrations, and demonstrate pro and con various political matters and issues of conscience. The Square's enduring vitality reflects Concord's determination to remain a living town.

Clockwise from the Colonial Inn around Monument Square:
Colonial Inn The Colonial Inn building (48 Monument Square) stands on land that was originally owned by the Reverend Peter Bulkeley (Concord's first minister and an ancestor of Ralph Waldo Emerson), later by the Wheeler and Minot families. The building consists of three old structures joined together.

Colonial Inn, ca. 1937, by George Shepard

Nineteenth-century storekeeper, businessman, and investor Daniel Shattuck once owned the leftmost and central portions of the building. The central section had served as Deacon John White's store, where young John Thoreau (Henry David's father) clerked and which Shattuck bought. (After working in White's employ, John Thoreau set himself up in business on Monument Square, running a store on the present Town House site in the building moved in 1850 to what is now 15 Monument Street in preparation for Town House construction.) Deacon White was a faithful observer of the Sabbath who demanded similar devotion in others. Although strict in this regard, he had a soft spot for the local children, to whom he gave New Year's presents of small books.

Built by James Minot, acquired in 1789 by cabinet maker Ammi White (whom local rumor has connected with the killing by hatchet of a British soldier wounded at the North Bridge on April 19, 1775), the rightmost section was occupied from 1800 by John Thoreau— grandfather of Henry David Thoreau—and his family. Henry Thoreau lived here part of the time he was a student at Harvard.

The three conjoined structures have provided food and lodging under the name "Colonial Inn" from early in the twentieth century.

Courthouse-Insurance Building The former Middlesex County courthouse at 34 Monument Square sits across Monument Street from the Thoreau section of the Colonial Inn. It was constructed in 1849 to replace a county courthouse erected in 1794, which burned. (In the 1880s, local historian Edward Jarvis described the 1794 courthouse as "a beautiful structure with a high tower on the top and . . . far more elegant and imposing than the present one.") When the county courts left Concord altogether in 1867, the newer courthouse was sold to the Town of Concord for a pittance. It then became the home of the Middlesex Mutual Fire Insurance Company. Today the building is used primarily for commercial purposes.

Town House Concord's Italianate brick Town House at 22 Monument Square is the first local municipal office building entirely separate from Middlesex County court facilities. Funds to build it were authorized at town meeting in 1850. Later that year, the town paid John Shepard Keyes for the property on which the Town House was to be constructed, and auctioned the building that then stood on the lot. Boston architect Richard Bond—whose other work included Lewis Wharf in Boston—designed the Town House. Alterations have been made to it several times.

The Town House has been a hub of municipal activity since 1851. During much of the nineteenth century, it also served as a center of Concord's social, cultural, and political life. In this building, Emerson spoke before the Concord Lyceum; Bronson Alcott (as Superintendent of Schools here) presided over school exhibitions; local people publicly observed a community Christmas celebration in 1853; fiery abolitionist John Brown spoke twice (in 1857 and 1859); and Brown's execution was mourned with solemn ceremony on December 2, 1859, through a program presented by the Reverend Grindall Reynolds of the First Parish, Emerson, Thoreau, Bronson Alcott, John Shepard Keyes, Frank Sanborn, and Ebenezer Rockwood Hoar.

Among the historical objects and artifacts in the Town House, visitors may be especially interested in the large painting *Memories of Antietam* by Philadelphia-born Concord artist Elizabeth Wentworth

City Hall [i.e. Town House], *1875, from card stereograph*

Roberts. Miss Roberts was the founder in 1917 of the Concord Art Association, to which at her death in 1927 she bequeathed the Ball House (now 37 Lexington Road, and still the association's home and gallery). She completed this massive group portrait of sixteen surviving Concord Civil War veterans in 1924. In 1928, the Concord Art Association offered *Memories of Antietam* to the Town of Concord as a gift, which the citizens of Concord voted to accept at town meeting in March 1929. It hangs in the public hearing room on the second floor of the Town House.

The Town House is normally open for public business Monday through Friday. (The hours of certain town departments and—occasionally—for the building as a whole may vary. Check the Town of Concord website at www.concordma.gov for more information.) Visitors may view *Memories of Antietam* when the second floor hearing room is not in use.

Together with the Soldiers' Monument on the Common—Concord's highly visible memorial to local men who died in the Civil War—*Memories of Antietam* reflects the value placed by the community on individual commitment and bravery in that conflict, and also the deep impact made here by the unprecedented loss of life it entailed.

Holy Family Church (St. Bernard's)-Universalist Meeting House

The building at 12 Monument Square—the corner of Bedford Street and Monument Square, across Bedford Street from the Town House—is now the church of the Roman Catholic Holy Family Parish. It was originally built as a Universalist meeting house. The First Universalist Society (Concord's third church) was organized in 1838. Its meeting house was built on Bedford Street and dedicated in 1840. In 1863, the Universalist church building was sold to Concord's Roman Catholic community and subsequently remodeled and turned to face Monument Square—its present orientation. For many years the structure served as the church for St. Bernard's Parish. In 2004, Our Lady Help of Christians Parish in West Concord was closed as part of the reconfiguration of the Archdiocese of Boston. St. Bernard's Parish was also closed, and the new Holy Family Parish—intended to draw members of both former parishes—was established at the site of St. Bernard's Church. The church building has been renovated several times since its first remodeling in the nineteenth century.

Hill Burying Ground The Hill Burying Ground is situated next to the Holy Family Church, where Lexington Road runs off from Monument Square. Its history is intertwined with the founding and settlement of Concord in the 1630s. The town's church was gathered in 1636 in Cambridge. Ministers Peter Bulkeley and John Jones were formally installed in 1637. The church's first meeting house was built on the hill on the opposite side of Lexington Road from the present location of the First Parish, above the burying ground, along the ridge where the earliest English settlers constructed primitive dug-out homes for protection from the elements. As was the general practice in seventeenth-century New England towns, the cemetery was located directly by the meeting house. Later, when a new and larger second meeting house was built across the road (1667–1673), the cemetery remained in operation in its original location.

There are nearly five hundred grave markers in the Hill Burying Ground. The earliest marked grave is that of Joseph Meriam, who died in 1677. But even though the cemetery holds no earlier markers, it was undoubtedly in use from Concord's settlement. Several theories have been offered as to why no markers survive from the forty-plus years following Concord's founding. Perhaps, in their preoccupation with

Hill Burying Ground, ca. 1925

carving a town out of wilderness, the early settlers simply had more pressing concerns than erecting gravestones. Or they may have feared trouble with the local Native population and preferred not to provide visible evidence of diminished strength. Or they may, in fact, have put up grave markers before 1677, but made them of a perishable material that did not survive the ravages of time and New England weather. In any event, Concord is not unique among New England towns in this absence of grave markers from the earliest years of its inhabitation.

The Hill Burying Ground is one of two cemeteries established in Concord in the seventeenth century. Together with the South Burying Ground on Main Street, it served the town's needs until the early nineteenth century, when space in both began to run out. (Opened on Bedford Street in 1823, a third cemetery—the predecessor of Sleepy Hollow Cemetery—was called the New Hill Burying Ground.)

Concord's earliest cemetery was still in active use when Amos Doolittle depicted it in one of the four famous Lexington and Concord images he engraved soon after April 19, 1775. His Plate II ("A View of the Town of Concord") shows Major Pitcairn and Lieutenant Colonel Smith standing in the cemetery, keeping an eye on the Colonial troops through a spyglass.

The gravestones in the Hill Burying Ground provide rich documentation of Concord's social history. The cemetery reflects life stories in a tangible and accessible form—the stories of the people buried here, those who mourned them, those who dug their graves, who wrote their epitaphs, who paid to have their monuments carved and hauled, artisans whose skill is evident in the ornamentation of those monuments, and the many people since the seventeenth century who have served in one capacity or another as caretakers, stewards, and interpreters of the place.

The graves and tombs in the Hill Burying Ground provide the final resting place for members of many of Concord's early and prominent families, among them Ball, Barrett, Blood, Brooks, Brown, Buttrick, Chandler, Clark, Farrar, Fletcher, Flint, Hartwell, Heald, Heywood, Hoar, Hosmer, Hubbard, Hunt, Melvin, Meriam, Minot, Potter, Stow, Temple, and Wheeler. The cemetery holds the graves of men whose names are synonymous with the beginnings of the Revolution at the North Bridge (James Barrett, John Buttrick, and alarm rider Reuben

Brown). It also enfolds the mortal remains of women prevented by the strictures of their time from playing a visible role in public life and of children who died too young to leave a mark on the world beyond family. First Parish ministers Daniel Bliss and Ezra Ripley are buried here, and a monument stands to William Emerson, whose body lies elsewhere. (Army chaplain at Ticonderoga, William Emerson died and was buried in Rutland, Vermont, some sixty years before his grandson Ralph Waldo Emerson settled permanently in Concord.)

The grave inscription that draws more attention than any other is that of John Jack (or Jack Barron), a pre-Revolutionary slave who bought his freedom. Daniel Bliss—a lawyer, loyalist, and son of minister Daniel Bliss—wrote the well-known epitaph on Jack's stone, thereby immortalizing a man who might otherwise have vanished from collective memory. (John Jack's grave marker is located at the rear of the Hill Burying Ground, near the property line between the Holy Family Church and the cemetery.)

Many of the predominantly slate markers in the Hill Burying Ground constitute fine examples of the stonecutter's work from Colonial times to the early Republic. Stones from various periods feature winged skulls, portraits, willows, urns, floral and geometric designs, and borders. Only a few bear the names of the makers. Concord's Department of Public Works (under which the Cemetery Department falls) has taken pains in recent years to ensure the documentation and preservation of this cultural resource.

The narrow entrance to the Hill Burying Ground is situated next to the Holy Family Church. From it the visitor proceeds up into the cemetery by a steep path, at the end of which (in the section of the cemetery farthest away from the Holy Family Church) stands an old brick powder house of uncertain vintage. Cemetery hours are from 7:00 A.M. until dusk daily, weather permitting. Visitors may not make rubbings from the stones in Concord's cemeteries. The genealogist or other researcher seeking a specific early grave might want to stop by the Concord Free Public Library Special Collections to check grave listings and cemetery maps rather than wander from grave to grave. Those with less directed interests may prefer simply to explore.

The Common and Soldiers' Monument   From Concord's Colonial beginnings, the grassed area in the middle of Monument Square has served as an important locus of town life and a mirror of community values. In the nineteenth century, Concord people often referred to it as "the Common." During this period, its purposes became increasingly memorial. Although an abortive attempt was made in 1825 to place here a monument to the events of April 19, 1775, the Civil War marked the real turning point in the use of the area.

Like towns and cities all over the country, Concord mourned local soldiers lost in the Civil War. The Concord Artillery (part of the Fifth Massachusetts Volunteer Militia) had entered the fray early, departing by train for Boston on April 19, 1861 (just a week after war broke out with the Confederate attack on Fort Sumter), and traveling thence to Washington. Two Concord companies spent much of the war in action. Several dozen Concord natives or residents perished over its course.

The Civil War ended in April 1865. The following year, Concord voted to erect a monument to honor its war dead and appointed a committee to make the necessary arrangements. A memorial obelisk forty-nine feet and six inches in height from the foundation was subsequently placed centrally on the Common in Monument Square, across from the strip of land between the courthouse building and the Town House. Designed by Boston artist and architect Hammatt Billings, the monument incorporated a stone taken from an abutment that had supported the Old North Bridge of April 19, 1775. (There was no bridge on the site of the North Bridge at the time the Soldiers' Monument was under construction.) The names of thirty-two men who "found here a birthplace, home or grave" were inscribed on a bronze plaque on the obelisk. Additions have since been made to the original list.

The Soldiers' Monument was dedicated on April 19, 1867. The ceremonies that day included an address by Ralph Waldo Emerson (a Concord resident and member of the town's twenty-five man Monument Committee, as well as a world-renowned author, lecturer, and philosopher) and brief remarks by visiting dignitaries George S. Boutwell and William Schouler. Judge John Shepard Keyes served as President of the Day.

Monument Square, showing Common,
Soldiers' Monument, and
(in distance) First Parish, 1909

Emerson opened his address by calling attention to the significance of April 19 as the anniversary both of the Concord Fight and of the day on which the troops had departed from Concord for Washington in 1861. He closed emotionally, invoking the higher purpose of the sacrifices made: "There are people who can hardly read the names on yonder bronze tablet, the mist so gathers in their eyes. Three of the names are of sons of one family. A gloom gathers on this assembly, composed as it is of kindred men and women, for, in many houses, the dearest and noblest is gone from their hearthstone. Yet it is tinged with light from heaven. A duty so severe has been discharged, and with such immense results of good, lifting private sacrifice to the sublime, that, though the cannon volleys have the sound of funeral echoes, they can yet hear through them the benedictions of their country and mankind."

The placement of Concord's Civil War memorial on the Common made the area the natural location for monuments to those who served and died in later wars. A boulder with a bronze marker was placed at the end of the Common closest to the Colonial Inn in memory of the three Concord men who died in the Spanish-American War (the War of 1898). In 1924, a permanent World War I memorial (a granite boulder with a bronze tablet bearing the names of local casualties) was situated at the opposite end of the Common, roughly across from the Town House. It was dedicated on May 25 (Memorial Day) of that year. Additionally, a memorial park was created across from the Common, at the corner of Main Street and Monument Square (opposite the Wright Tavern) to honor Concordians who served and died in conflicts beginning with World War II.

Flagpole The flagpole on the small traffic circle in Monument Square is successor to the liberty pole that stood with flag flying on April 19, 1775, on the nearby ridge above the Hill Burying Ground. Coming into Concord that day, British troops cut down the liberty pole, a defiant symbol of political protest and self-determination. A pole was later restored to the top of the hill, and after America gained independence, the banner that flew from it was the national flag. Nineteenth-century Concord social historian Edward Jarvis reported that the town dug and carted away so much gravel from the hill for road repair that the flagpole eventually became unstable, and was consequently moved down into the Square, where—despite the necessity of replacing it from time to time (for example, after the Hurricane of 1938)—it remains a prominent feature today.

Wright Tavern Two hundred and fifty years old in 1997, the Wright Tavern is located at the corner of Main Street and Lexington Road, across from the former Middlesex Hotel site. Over time, it has become permanently associated with the name of Amos Wright, who neither built nor owned the structure but who happened to be the tavernkeeper there on April 19, 1775—Concord's great day in Revolutionary history. The local minute men gathered at the tavern early that day. Later, when the king's troops reached Concord, Lieutenant Colonel Smith and Major Pitcairn used it as British headquarters. Visitors and local people alike are familiar with the anecdotal story of Pitcairn at the tavern, stirring his drink with his finger and threatening to do the same with Yankee blood.

The land on which the Wright Tavern stands was first owned by the Reverend Peter Bulkeley, next by Timothy and George Wheeler, then (through the bequest of Timothy Wheeler) by the Town of Concord. In 1747, the town sold the lot to Ephraim Jones, a Concord selectman and town clerk, who built the tavern. In 1751, he sold it to Thomas Munroe of Lexington, who failed to make it financially successful. It was sold in 1766 to Daniel Taylor, who kept it until 1775, when Samuel Swan bought it. During Swan's ownership, a wing with an oven was added and a bakery business started. Following the custom of the period, under its early owners, the town's selectmen met, dined, and drank at the tavern at municipal expense.

The Wright Tavern building was later owned by bakers Thomas Safford and Francis Jarvis. Safford sold his interest to Jarvis in 1795. After the Jarvis family sold the building (1832), the Wright Tavern was occupied by a series of tenants. Finally, Reuben Rice and Ebenezer Rockwood Hoar—two prominent and civic-minded local residents— bought it and, in the 1880s, conveyed it to the First Parish in Concord on condition that the building not be taken down.

Today, the tavern building is a National Historic Landmark. It provides office space for the First Parish, business space, and a home for the Wright Tavern Center for Spiritual Renewal, which was founded in 1997 to nurture spirit, enrich daily life, and encourage the personal development of members of the First Parish and of the local and surrounding communities.

Wright's Tavern, Halt of British Officers upon their march into Concord, *1875*
(from card stereograph)

Veterans' Memorial-Middlesex Hotel Site   The property at the corner of Main Street and Monument Square, opposite the Wright Tavern, has been under municipal ownership since 1900. Today, a memorial park on it honors Concord soldiers who died in World War II, the Korean War, and the conflicts in the Dominican Republic and Vietnam. A marker to World War II casualties was placed on the site in the late 1940s. In 1997, two separate markers for those lost in wars since World War II were erected and landscaping improvements made through a concerted community effort. The revamped memorial was dedicated late in 1997.

This park occupies the former site of the Middlesex Hotel, which provided food, drink, and lodging for lawyers, litigants, and witnesses on court days while Concord was still a shire town (county seat). Attendees of the Middlesex Agricultural Society's annual fall Cattle Show lodged and dined here. Workers in the shops on Concord's Mill Dam stopped in for a quick drink during their day. The hotel accommodated large dinners and dances, including the lavish military balls of the Concord Artillery, and a local dancing school. It offered rest and refreshment to teamsters hauling loads over long distances, and food and drink (paid for by the Town of Concord) to selectmen and other local officials meeting to transact municipal business. It was also a stop for passenger and mail stages before the coming of the railroad (1844) led to the decline of the stagecoach as a form of transportation.

Hotelkeeper John Richardson arrived in Concord in the late 1770s and ran a tavern in the building now known as the Catholic rectory (70 Monument Square). He soon exchanged that structure and some land behind it for the next property south (closer to the Mill Dam), then owned by Middlesex County. Richardson expanded the former county building on his new lot into the successful operation eventually known as the Middlesex Hotel.

The old Dr. Timothy Minot House and the adjacent county-owned building that Richardson acquired and renovated stood on property that in the seventeenth century had belonged to Concord founder Peter Bulkeley and where the retroactive purchase of Concord land by English settlers from the Native Americans was signed in 1637, under "Jethro's Tree." (The Minot House is seen in Amos Doolittle's depiction of the Monument Square area in 1775, engraved just a few years before John Richardson came to Concord.)

Richardson operated the hotel himself for a time, then placed it under the care of a series of managers. He moved from Concord in the first decade of the nineteenth century and in 1825 sold the hotel to Thomas D. Wesson and Gershom Fay, who ran it together for a few years. Fay sold his interest to Wesson, a genial and well-liked man who during the hotel's heyday (1825–1845) clashed with local people only over the issue of temperance. In 1839, Sam Staples—Thoreau's jailer in 1846—married Wesson's daughter. Staples was barkeeper in and, for a while, manager of Wesson's establishment.

The Middlesex Hotel burned in 1845. Against advice, Wesson built a new hotel on the location of, and similar to, the one that had gone up in flames. (In constructing a porch on the east side, he used remnants of the cornerstone of the unfinished monument to the Concord Fight placed on the Common in 1825.) Despite his optimism, he was unable to run the new place profitably. From its reopening until its ultimate closing in 1882, the Middlesex passed through a rapid succession of owners and managers. The convenience and speed of railroad travel decimated business, as did the loss to Lowell by the late 1840s of two terms of the Court of Common Pleas. (The remaining courts were removed from Concord in 1867.) Toward the end of the hotel's operation, the town was unwilling to allow the serving of liquor there. The coup de grâce was delivered in 1881, when the Middlesex suffered another major fire.

Following the downward spiral of its final thirty-plus years of operation, the abandoned Middlesex Hotel stood a decaying hulk in Concord Center for nearly two decades. Finally, in 1900, four community-oriented Concordians (Stedman Buttrick, Edward Waldo Emerson, Richard F. Barrett, and Prescott Keyes) bought it and sold it to the Town of Concord. The site was designated for municipal purposes as part of the town's celebration of the one hundred and twenty-fifth anniversary of the Concord Fight, and the building was finally demolished.

Holy Family Rectory-County House   The Catholic rectory at 70 Monument Square is not a tourist site. Nevertheless, its history is significant and interconnected with that of other buildings on the Square.

The historical importance of the Holy Family Rectory lies primarily in its ownership by Middlesex County in the late eighteenth century and the first half of the nineteenth. About 1780, tavern-keeper John Richardson either constructed what is now the rectory building or renovated an earlier structure on the lot it occupies. In 1789, he traded it and some land behind it to Middlesex County for the corner lot. The county converted the building Richardson had conveyed to it into living quarters for county officers.

Appointed jailer, Richardson lived in part of the building that he had traded to the county. Later occupants of the place included William Hildreth (who served as sheriff) and jailers Abel Moore and Sam Staples.

Part of the County House was leased out to tenants. Cabinet and pencil maker William Munroe (Monroe), Sr., rented part of it in the first decade of the nineteenth century. William Munroe, Jr.—William Sr.'s first child and, in the 1870s, the founding benefactor of the Concord Free Public Library—was born here in 1806.

In 1867, when the last of the Middlesex County courts moved from Concord, the county conveyed all its property to the town, which sold the County House to the Archdiocese of Boston in 1868. Subsequently extensively renovated, the building has served not only as the Catholic rectory but also, before Monument Hall was built next door (60/62 Monument Square) early in the twentieth century, as a parish hall for St. Bernard's Parish.

County Jail Site The tavern John Richardson traded became the new County House, where jailers and sheriffs lived, and the property diagonally behind it (between the Middlesex Hotel and the County House) was used for a stone county jail. This was the jail in which Henry David Thoreau spent one night in the summer of 1846 for nonpayment of the poll tax in resistance against the Mexican-American War. Abolitionists detested the war as an attempt by the "slave power" to extend the geographical range of slavery. There are no surviving images of the stone jail, which is long gone, but Thoreau, in his lecture-turned-essay "Civil Disobedience," provided a description of it and—more significantly—his personal perspective on his experience there:

I was put into a jail once . . . for one night; and, as I stood
considering the walls of solid stone, two or three feet thick,
the door of wood and iron, a foot thick, and the iron grating
which strained the light, I could not help being struck with
the foolishness of that institution which treated me as if I
were mere flesh and blood and bones, to be locked up . . .
I saw that if there was a wall of stone between me and my
townsmen, there was a still more difficult one to climb or
break through, before they could get to be as free as I was.

When the last of the county courts left Concord in the 1860s, the jail
was demolished and stones from it were reused (some of them in a wall
at Sleepy Hollow Cemetery).

Masonic Temple   The Masonic Hall at 58 Monument Square was
built as a public schoolhouse in 1820. Located in the Center District of
the seven-district school system then operating in Concord, this brick
schoolhouse replaced a wooden predecessor that was built in 1799
and burned late in 1819. Proposing to use the new school building
for meeting space, the local Corinthian Lodge of Freemasons contributed funding for its construction. When the building was completed,
the school was located on the first floor, the Freemasons' hall on
the second.

     The school served as a grammar school and a high school. Henry
David Thoreau briefly taught here in 1837. (Opposed to corporal pun-
ishment as a means of discipline, he quickly resigned.) Between 1844
and 1852, the Freemasons rented their quarters in the structure and
paid for the use of space there for their own then-intermittent meetings. In 1851, the grammar and high schools were relocated to the
newly-constructed Town House, and the brick schoolhouse was renovated to serve Fire Department purposes.

     In 1871, the Masons sold their interest in the building to the
town, which later sold it to a private owner. The Corinthian Lodge
met elsewhere for a time, but returned to the schoolhouse in 1882,
purchasing it back in 1909. Still home to the Corinthian Lodge,
the building is sometimes rented by other organizations for lectures
and meetings.

Monument Street

The lower portion of the present Monument Street (the section near-est Monument Square) formed part of Concord's seventeenth-century road system. The Old Groton Road ran along the current track of Monument Street from Monument Square as far as the access road to the North Bridge, where it approached and crossed the river and con-tinued on up the hill on the opposite side, running toward what is now Lowell Road and connecting with other roads on the way to Groton. On April 19, 1775, British troops followed the Groton Road from the center of Concord to the North Bridge and from there toward the Bar-rett farmhouse to search for military supplies and weapons.

Notoriously susceptible to weather damage and requiring fre-quent repair, the North Bridge was dismantled in 1793 and the sur-rounding road and bridge system reconfigured, creating a new section of what is now known as Monument Street and the first bridge to stand at the site of the present Flint's Bridge. The upper part of Monument Street (beyond the Old Manse and the avenue to the Battle Monument) was known in earlier times as the River Road to Carlisle.

Historic structures line both the lower and upper reaches of Monument Street. Most of these buildings remain in use as private homes and are not open to visitors. Nevertheless, two major Concord historic sites (the Old Manse and the North Bridge Unit of the Minute Man National Historical Park) are located on the lower portion of the street, making it a key tourist route. These sites are accessible on foot from Monument Square. For those who simply want to take advan-tage of a fine day for a good walk, the longer stretch of Monument Street beyond the avenue to the North Bridge offers fine farm and river vistas and wooded areas, providing ample opportunity to enjoy the Concord landscape.

The visitor proceeds from Monument Square to Monument Street at the Colonial Inn end of the Square, with the Inn to the left and the former courthouse building to the right.

Grave of the Third British Soldier   Immediately on passing from Monument Square to Monument Street, a small marker sits on the grass at the edge of the courthouse side of the street. This monument (a

natural boulder with incised lettering) was placed in 2000 in memory
of one of three British soldiers who died as a result of wounds sustained
at the North Bridge on April 19, 1775. A stone marker stands near the
North Bridge site of the Concord Fight to honor two British soldiers
who fell and were buried there. A third soldier was carried still living
from the field, later died, and was buried in or on the outskirts of the
present Monument Square. His grave was unmarked until the approach
of the two hundred and twenty-fifth anniversary of the Concord Fight
prompted private efforts to arrange and fund a memorial. The ceremony to dedicate the marker was held on November 12, 2000.

The Cottage-Country Store-Keyes House At 15 Monument Street—
next to the Colonial Inn and across from the Grave of the Third British
Soldier—stands what used to be the Country Store of Concord. Local
old-timers and out-of-towners alike fondly recall this place.

The structure that housed the Country Store in the twentieth
century was built in 1780 on Main Street and subsequently moved
to Monument Square, where it stood when Henry Thoreau's father
John ran a store business in it. It became the property of lawyer John
Shepard Keyes, who moved it in the mid-nineteenth century to permit
construction of the Town House. Keyes and his wife, children, and
widowed mother occupied it in its new location.

For decades beginning in 1941, the Country Store sold penny
candy, jams, casual clothing, and gifts to an appreciative clientele and
conducted an extensive mail order business. The store was established
by F. H. Trumbull, later taken over by his daughter and son-in-law,
Mary and William Locke. It passed out of Locke ownership in the
1980s. Much renovated and named "The Cottage," it is now part of
the Colonial Inn complex.

Elisha Jones House (Bullet Hole House) Proceeding up Monument
Street from the Square, the visitor will pass the historic Elisha Jones
House, or "Bullet Hole House," on the right, at 242 Monument. At
the outset of the Revolution, Jones concealed provincial stores in a
shed on his property. On April 19, 1775, he and his family hid in
the cellar of their house as the British marched to the North Bridge
and stopped along the way to refresh themselves at Jones's well. Later,
hearing the shots fired at the bridge, the Joneses rushed up from the

Elisha Jones House (Bullet Hole House) and view down Monument Street toward center of Concord, 1890s

cellar. According to family and local tradition, as the British troops retreated from the bridge after the Concord Fight, a regular caught sight of Elisha standing in the shed and fired at him, missing his target but leaving a hole in the structure. (Twentieth-century historians have questioned the credibility of the story.) The shed was later moved and joined to the house as an ell. The hole allegedly made by the British musket ball is still visible today near the ell doorway, under protective plexiglass. The house was owned by Jones and Barrett family members until the mid-1860s, when it was purchased by Judge John Shepard Keyes, who extensively renovated and expanded it, and also fixed in local consciousness the story of Elisha Jones's brush with a British soldier. Now part of the Minute Man National Historical Park, the house is not open to visitors.

Old Manse   The Old Manse—one of Concord's most historic houses and a National Historic Landmark—stands across from the Bullet Hole House, just before the avenue leading to the North Bridge, at 269 Monument Street, set back from the road. The Concord Fight of April 19, 1775, took place within sight of the Manse's occupants. Home in earlier times to Concord ministers and to two of the town's renowned nineteenth-century authors, the Manse has belonged to the Trustees of Reservations since 1939.

William Emerson—a descendant of Concord founder and first minister Peter Bulkeley, minister of the church in Concord from 1765 to 1776, and grandfather of Ralph Waldo Emerson—built the Manse on what started out during English settlement of the area as Blood family property and in time passed to the Browns. The deed documenting the conveyance of the property from David Brown to William Emerson is dated April 16, 1770. From William Emerson's time until signed over to the Trustees of Reservations, the Manse remained in the hands of Emersons, Ripleys, and Ripley descendants (Simmonses, Thayers, and Ameses).

Daniel Bliss—Ralph Waldo Emerson's great-grandfather—was the minister in Concord from 1739 until his death in 1764. A New Light Congregationalist caught up in the Great Awakening revivalism preached by Jonathan Edwards, Bliss twice welcomed English evangelist George Whitefield to Concord, in 1741 and 1764. During Bliss's ministry, there was considerable discord among his parishioners over his evangelical fervor, leading to the departure from the established church of some who chose to worship separately.

William Emerson, who served as a supply preacher here after Daniel Bliss's death, was chosen in 1765 to succeed Bliss as minister of the Concord church. He married Bliss's daughter Phebe in 1766, and in 1770 moved Phebe and their first child, William (Ralph Waldo's father) into the Manse. After the move, they had four more children—including Mary Moody Emerson, later a great intellectual influence on her nephew Waldo. The Reverend Emerson was a popular as well as an eloquent minister. A champion of political liberty, he was one of Concord's Revolutionary leaders. When the Provincial Congress met in Concord in October of 1774, he officiated as chaplain. On August 16, 1776, just after the birth of his fifth child, he left Concord to serve as army chaplain at Fort Ticonderoga. He never returned. He became sick, and died at Rutland, Vermont, while trying to come home. A memorial to him stands in the Hill Burying Ground.

After William Emerson's death in 1776, his widow and family stayed on in the Manse. Ezra Ripley—minister in Concord for a remarkable sixty-three years, from 1778 to 1841—was head of the Manse household from his marriage in 1780 to the widowed Phebe Bliss Emerson. As a senior at Harvard, Ripley had stayed in Concord during the school's removal here in 1775 and 1776. This early personal association with Concord gave him a life-long interest in the town's place in history, and especially in the story of the Concord Fight and in the people and sites associated with it. At the Manse, the Ripleys raised William and Phebe's children (with the exception of Mary Moody Emerson, who was raised by relatives), and three of their own. Ripley's senior by eleven years, Phebe died sixteen years before her second husband.

Patriarch though Ezra Ripley was, he was loved as well as respected in Concord, known as a generous, sympathetic, and sincere man, if sometimes harsh; direct, practical, sociable, fond of company and conversation, but also opinionated and not particularly intellectual. Over the course of his ministry, the First Parish gradually grew away from its original Congregational Calvinism toward Unitarianism. Ripley was not antagonistic to the liberalization of his church, but he remained old-fashioned in his attachment to traditional forms and observances. During Ripley's residence in the Manse, the house was always open to friends and family.

William Emerson, the oldest child of William and Phebe Bliss Emerson and a minister in Boston, died prematurely in 1811, leaving his wife—Ruth Haskins Emerson—six children to raise and educate. Ralph Waldo Emerson was the fourth of the couple's eight

Old Manse, ca. 1875 (from card stereograph)

children, two of whom died before their father. Ezra Ripley welcomed William's widow and the young Emersons—his step-grandchildren—as visitors to the Manse, and shared his knowledge and love of Concord with them. Ruth Emerson and her children stayed at the Manse for an extended period from November 1814 until the following April.

Having spent time at the Manse as a boy, Ralph Waldo Emerson moved with his mother to the house in 1834. (They were Ezra Ripley's boarders.) Soon afterward, Emerson wrote emotionally in his journal, "Hail to the quiet fields of my fathers! Not wholly unattended by supernatural friendship & favor let me come hither. Bless my purposes as they are simple and virtuous . . . Henceforth I design not to utter any speech, poem, or book that is not entirely & peculiarly my work." Emerson's hereditary attachment to Concord sustained and nurtured him as he worked at the Manse on his long-developing book, *Nature*.

Following Ezra Ripley's death in 1841, the Manse was rented out. In July of 1842, author Nathaniel Hawthorne married aspiring artist Sophia Amelia Peabody— who along with her sisters Elizabeth Palmer Peabody and Mary Tyler Peabody (Mann) formed the triune later dubbed "the Peabody sisters of Salem"—and brought his bride to the Manse to live. Before the newlyweds moved in, Elizabeth Hoar (fiancée of Ralph Waldo Emerson's brother Charles, who died in 1836; an intimate of the entire Emerson family; and a learned woman) and Cynthia Thoreau (Henry David Thoreau's mother) prepared the house for their arrival.

The Hawthornes were blissfully happy in the Manse. They delighted in the beauty of the Concord landscape and in the amusements it offered. Una, the first of their three children, was born here in 1844. Moreover, although shy, Hawthorne enjoyed the company of Thoreau, Ellery Channing, and other local residents, and of out-of-town visitors as well. The couple stayed here until 1845. They returned to Concord twice again, but not to the Manse. (The Wayside on Lexington Road was their later home). Not widely recognized as an author until after his first sojourn in Concord, Nathaniel Hawthorne drew attention to the Manse through the collection of stories titled *Mosses from an Old Manse* (1846), the opening piece in which begins:

> *Between two tall gate-posts of rough hewn stone (the gate itself having fallen from its hinges, at some unknown epoch), we beheld the grey front of the old parsonage . . . The glimmering shadows, that lay half asleep between the door of the house and the public highway, were a kind of spiritual medium, seen through which, the edifice had not quite the aspect of belonging to the material world.*

Drawn though Hawthorne was to the otherworldliness of the Manse, and contented though he and Sophia were while living here, the impending return to Concord of Samuel Ripley—Ezra Ripley's son and a minister in Waltham—made their departure inevitable.

Samuel Ripley retired from his Waltham pastorate and came back to the Manse, his childhood home, in 1846. His wife Sarah Alden Bradford Ripley—a learned, thoughtful woman highly respected by Emerson and his intellectual comrades—remained at the Manse after Samuel's sudden death in 1847. Married to Samuel Ripley in 1818, she had raised seven children and assisted her husband in teaching and taking care of the boys at the boarding school he ran in Waltham—a task for which she was admirably prepared. As a child, Mrs. Ripley had learned Latin and Greek—subjects unusual for a girl of the time. A life-long practitioner of self-culture, she became proficient in modern languages as well as ancient (she knew German), and in literature, science (she was renowned as a botanist), mathematics, history, and philosophy. She attended some of Margaret Fuller's conversations in Boston and was invited to the so-called Transcendental Club. Rational and skeptical, she had difficulty reconciling her acute observations with orthodox religion.

During Sarah Ripley's residence in the Manse, her grandson Edward Emerson Simmons spent time in the old house. Artistically inclined, young Simmons decorated walls in the Manse with his sketches. In maturity, he was a prominent artist—a muralist whose wall and ceiling paintings graced public and private buildings across America, who worked in other media as well, and who belonged to a group of American impressionists (also including Frank W. Benson, Childe Hassam, and Willard Metcalf) known as "The Ten." Simmons depicted the Concord Fight in a well-known mural in the Massachusetts State House.

Sophia Ripley—one of Sarah and Samuel Ripley's daughters—married James B. Thayer, and their youngest daughter Sarah married John B. Ames. When the house became the property of the Trustees of Reservations in 1939, it had been continuously owned and almost continuously occupied by Emersons and their heirs for nearly one hundred and seventy years.

At the Old Manse, visitors may view not only the furnishings and personal effects of generations of the house's occupants, but also a recreation of the 1842 vegetable garden planted by Thoreau for the Hawthornes and a reconstructed late nineteenth-century boathouse on the Concord River directly behind the house. The Manse is open to visitors from mid-April through the end of October, with regular hours Monday through Saturday and more limited hours Sundays and holidays. For information about hours, fees, tours, programs, the museum shop, and other details, consult the Manse's website at http://www.thetrustees.org/places-to-visit/greater-boston/old-manse.html. The phone number is (978) 369-3909.

The Robbins House Dedicated to the African-American and anti-slavery history of Concord, The Robbins House is situated just up Monument Street beyond the Old Manse, on the opposite side of the road, at the edge of the parking lot across from the entrance to Minute Man National Historical Park. In the nineteenth century, the house was home to several generations of African-American Concordians. It has been moved twice, in 1871 from its original site on the Great Meadows to Bedford Street and in 2011 from Bedford Street to its current location. For visitor information, consult The Robbins House website at http://www.robbinshouse.org.

North Bridge Area
Minute Man National Historical Park In 1955, anticipating the approaching bicentennial of the American Revolution, the United States Congress formed the Boston National Historic Sites Commission, which considered the preservation of important local historical landmarks. The Commission's *Interim Report . . . Pertaining to the Lexington-Concord Battle Road* resulted in the

creation by Act of Congress of Minute Man National Historical Park in Concord, Lincoln, and Lexington in September 1959. United States Senator Leverett Saltonstall (former governor of Massachusetts) and state representatives Edith Nourse Rogers, Thomas P. ("Tip") O'Neill, and John McCormack were instrumental in founding the Park. Active outreach and programming began with the introduction of site interpretation at the North Bridge in 1963. Formal ceremonies marking its establishment and the dedication of what was then called the Battle Road Visitor Center (now the Minute Man Visitor Center) were held in 1976.

Fifty years old in 2009, Minute Man National Historical Park now draws more than a million visitors annually. It works to preserve the built and natural landscape of the area and offers a range of programs to foster understanding of the Concord Fight, the events surrounding it, and the people who lived it. Park rangers, interpreters in period garb, and volunteers all participate in interpretive activities. Encompassing more than nine hundred acres, Minute Man is divided into three units: the North Bridge Unit, the Wayside Unit, and the Battle Road Unit.

Following goals and objectives expressed in a 1989 general management plan, in recent years the National Park Service has devoted significant resources to restoring and rehabilitating the rural landscape along the Battle Road and to enhancing appreciation of traditional agriculture practices and land use patterns. The provision of trails for walking and bicycling—including the 5.5-mile Battle Road Trail—has formed part of this effort.

The visitor approaches the North Bridge Unit of the park from Monument Street, taking a left down a footpath just beyond the field next to the Old Manse, soon reaching the Battle Monument, the grave of two British soldiers who died on April 19, 1775, the reconstructed North Bridge, and—on the opposite bank of the Concord River— Daniel Chester French's *Minute Man* statue. By agreement between the Town of Concord and the Park Service, the former maintains ownership of the Battle Monument, the North Bridge, and the *Minute Man*.

For visitors' convenience, free parking is available in a lot across Monument Street from the footpath. There are restrooms on the approach to the bridge, on the right-hand side just beyond the entrance to the footpath. Following the path across the bridge, past the *Minute Man* statue, and up the hill beyond, the visitor will come to the North Bridge Visitor Center in the Buttrick Mansion at 174 Liberty Street (a former residence built in 1911), which offers a Liberty Street parking lot, an interpretive video and displays, a bookstore, and panoramic river and landscape views. (Some visitors may prefer to park in the Liberty Street lot and approach the bridge and surrounding monuments from there rather than from Monument Street.) Before it became National Park Service property, under the ownership of a descendant of John Buttrick of Concord Fight fame, the Buttrick estate was well-known for its extensive, well-tended iris gardens (no longer maintained).

Acquired by the park in 1966, the Major John Buttrick House at 231 Liberty Street (across the road from the Buttrick Mansion) was constructed early in the eighteenth century and was the home of Major John Buttrick, who commanded the Colonial troops on April 19, 1775. It now serves as an educational, programming, and meeting facility.

For more information about Minute Man National Historical Park, visit the Web pages at http://www.nps.gov/mima/index.htm, or contact park headquarters at (978) 369-6993.

Battle Monument Just before the North Bridge, the footpath reaches the Battle Monument. The history of the monument is closely related to that of the bridge. From 1793—when the weather-beaten bridge was dismantled—until 1874, no bridge stood on the site where the Concord Fight had taken place. Rather than rebuilding on a spot vulnerable to the elements and requiring frequent repair, the town erected a new bridge (Flint's Bridge) a short distance downstream and relocated the road that had run on the west side of the river to the east side. The Reverend Ezra Ripley asked for and was given the abandoned right-of-way adjacent to his Old Manse property from Monument Street to the site of the bridge.

The approaching fiftieth anniversary of the Concord Fight turned the attention of local people to erecting a monument to the event. Although the North Bridge area was historically resonant, on April 19,

1825, a cornerstone was laid in the town center, in Monument Square. The location was unpopular and no further progress was made on the monument. After a couple of years, the stone was cracked by a fire started by vandals and the plan of locating the monument in the center of town was abandoned.

At town meeting in March 1834, Ezra Ripley's proposal "respecting a site or piece of ground for the erection of a Monument in commemoration of the Great Events at Concord North Bridge on the 19th of April 1775" was raised. The town subsequently accepted Ripley's offer to hand back the right-of-way he had been given forty years earlier so that a proper monument to the Concord Fight could be put up where the event had actually taken place.

The Battle Monument was erected in 1836 on the east side of the river, on ground from which British troops had faced the Colonial rebels, who had stood on the west side. A twenty-five-foot obelisk of Westford granite with a white marble slab, it was designed by Solomon Willard (designer also of the Bunker Hill Monument, then still under construction). Although others were later credited with the inscription on the slab, Dr. Edward Jarvis actually wrote it.

Emerson composed his famous "Concord Hymn" for the dedication of the monument on July 4, 1837, when the poem was sung to the tune of the Old Hundredth. There was, ironically, no "rude bridge that arched the flood" at the time. A new bridge was constructed in 1874, when a cedar structure was put up for the 1875 centennial celebration of the Concord Fight. In 1838, two double rows of trees were planted along the path from the road to the monument to enhance the stateliness of the approach.

Grave of the British Soldiers To the left of the Battle Monument when facing the Concord River, adjacent to the stone wall separating the Old Manse property from the North Bridge area, the visitor will find the grave of two British soldiers who were buried where they fell on April 19, 1775. Their burial site was later marked through two private gifts. Over the years, considerable misinformation has circulated about the donation of the stone posts and iron chains enclosing the site and about the large stone slab on which lines of verse by James Russell Lowell are carved. (Even the 1959 *Interim Report of the Boston Historic Sites Commission* misstates the facts.) However, the persistent sleuthing of a determined independent historian finally established that the posts and chains were set in place not by English people from Waltham at the time of the centennial celebration of the Concord Fight in 1875, as has often been asserted, but rather in 1877, as the gift of English-born Boston investor Herbert Radclyffe. The slab was given in 1910 by philanthropist Peter Chardon Brooks of West Medford, Massachusetts. Regardless of how and when the grave of the British soldiers came to be marked, lines of poetry by James Russell Lowell provide a suitably moving memorial to the men who lie there: "They came three thousand miles and died, / To keep the past upon its throne. / Unheard beyond the ocean tide, / Their English mother made her moan."

North Bridge The arched wooden bridge depicted in Amos Doolittle's 1775 engraving "The Engagement at the North Bridge" is iconic. But the North Bridge (or Great Bridge, as it was earlier known) has been transformed many times since first built in the mid-seventeenth century. The structure that stood on April 19, 1775, was one in a series of bridges to span the Concord River at the site where it stood. Subject to the ravages of the seasonally rising river and to storm damage as well, the North Bridge has repeatedly been repaired and rebuilt throughout its long history.

In her *North Bridge Neighbors* (a 1964 report prepared for Minute Man National Historical Park), Concord historian Ruth R. Wheeler wrote, "The Great Bridge is older than the town records." Rebuilt in 1660, it required frequent replanking and other maintenance measures. The causeway that provided access to it in times of high water and a stone wall built to protect private property from careless passersby on their way to and from the bridge also had to be kept up.

In 1793, in accordance with a town meeting vote, the bridge that stood in 1775 was taken down, the road rerouted, and a new stone bridge (Flint's Bridge) built downstream. The structure dismantled in 1793 was the last purely functional—as opposed to commemorative—bridge on the original site. Eighty years later, another bridge was built at the former location of the old North Bridge. In 1874, an ornate Victorian affair in cedar, with gazebos, was erected for the

1875 centennial celebration of the Concord Fight. That bridge washed out in 1888 and was rebuilt more simply, in heavy oak, in 1889. The 1889 bridge in turn washed out in 1908 and was replaced in 1909 with a cement version (intended to accommodate automobile traffic), which was damaged by storm and flood in 1955.

In September 1956, a few years before Minute Man National Historical Park was formed, a new wooden bridge (similar to the structure shown in Doolittle's 1775 engraving) was dedicated. When the 1956 bridge was refurbished in 2005, its structural supports were retained but the wooden planking and rails were replaced.

Since construction of the Victorian bridge in 1874, the Town of Concord has used successive commemorative versions of the North Bridge for public ceremonies in remembrance of the Concord Fight. President Ulysses S. Grant and members of his cabinet did Concord

1874 version of the North Bridge, ca. 1875, from card stereograph

Daniel Chester French's Minute Man, *ca. 1895, by Alfred Winslow Hosmer*

the honor of attending the observances at the bridge during the 1875 centennial. (George William Curtis was the keynote speaker then, and Ralph Waldo Emerson delivered brief remarks that constituted the last of his many public addresses in Concord over the course of his long residence here.) A hundred years later, President Gerald R. Ford addressed a vast crowd from a platform adjacent to the bridge.

Now, each year on and around Patriots' Day, the Town of Concord's Public Ceremonies and Celebrations Committee and Minute Man National Historical Park organize events (including a parade and reenactments) at the North Bridge and in the surrounding area to commemorate the Concord Fight. For more information about Patriots' Day in Concord, visit the website of the Concord Chamber of Commerce at http://www.concordchamberofcommerce.org/.

Minute Man *Statue* The issue of a truly appropriate commemorative location for a monument to April 19, 1775, was not resolved until Daniel Chester French's *Minute Man* was placed on the west bank of the river—the "American side"—and unveiled at the centennial celebration of the Concord Fight in 1875. The *Minute Man* was placed on the spot where Isaac Davis of Acton was killed and where later grew a bush metaphorically compared to the Biblical "burning bush" of Exodus.

In his will, Concordian Ebenezer Hubbard (who died in 1871) left the Town of Concord $1,000 to erect a monument on the bank of the Concord River which Colonial forces had occupied in 1775, opposite from the "British side," where the Battle Monument stood. Stedman Buttrick subsequently deeded a small piece of land on which the proposed monument might be located. A committee was formed to consider Hubbard's bequest and, at the 1873 town meeting, recommended that it and Buttrick's gift be accepted, that a statue of a minute man be erected and a bridge providing access to it constructed, and that the dedication of the monument take place on April 19, 1875, the centennial anniversary of the Concord Fight.

Young Concord artist Daniel Chester French (born in New Hampshire in 1850) was selected for the job. French advised that the statue—his first public commission—be made of bronze rather than granite, which had been suggested by the town committee managing the Hubbard bequest. Distinguished Concord resident Ebenezer Rockwood Hoar—a judge, Attorney General of the United States in the cabinet of President Ulysses S. Grant from 1869 to 1870, and a representative in the United States Congress from 1873 to 1875— deeply felt the importance of the upcoming centennial. At his urging, Congress gave the Town of Concord ten condemned brass cannon for use in creating the proposed statue. The Act of Congress dedicating the cannon for this purpose was signed by President Grant on April 22, 1874. French's plaster model was used in casting the bronze statue at the Ames Manufacturing Company in Chicopee, Massachusetts.

The first verse of Ralph Waldo Emerson's moving "Concord Hymn"—composed for the dedication of the Battle Monument in 1837—is incised on the base of the *Minute Man:* "By the rude bridge that arched the flood, / Their flag to April's breeze unfurled, / Here once the embattled farmers stood, / And fired the shot heard round the world."

French's *Minute Man* quickly became a widely-recognized symbol of bravery, independence, and patriotism. After its unveiling (which the sculptor was unable to attend), French went on to a highly visible career as one of America's most successful public artists. His later work included the seated Lincoln unveiled in 1922 at the Lincoln Memorial in Washington, D.C.

Musterfield   Heading from the Buttrick Mansion south down Liberty Street (toward Lowell Road), the visitor will pass a tablet on the right. This stone marks the musterfield where the Colonial minute and militia companies formed before marching to the North Bridge on April 19, 1775.

Concord itself had two minute and two militia companies. In all, a total of four to five hundred Colonials—Concord's men and those who marched from nearby towns—faced the British regulars at the North Bridge. The British expeditionary force to Concord was seven or eight hundred strong, but the number of British soldiers actually present at the North Bridge under Captain Walter Laurie's command was in the vicinity of one hundred and fifteen men—perhaps a quarter the size of the Colonial presence. (In Colonial times, New England towns regularly maintained militia companies and kept them in training for whatever threats to public safety they might be required to quell, while minute companies were formed specifically to respond on short notice to particular emergencies.)

From the vantage point of the musterfield, the local troops observed smoke rising from the town center, where the British were burning cannon carriages they had found. Alarmed, Joseph Hosmer asked his now-famous question, "Will you let them burn the town down?" Colonel James Barrett subsequently ordered his men to march toward the bridge and the waiting British regulars, warning them not to fire first. Before leaving the musterfield, the provincials were ordered to discard possibly defective gunflints to ensure the success of their fire in battle. The discarded flints were found here in the twentieth century. (Some were given to the Concord Antiquarian Society, now known as the Concord Museum.)

Continuing on past the musterfield brings the visitor to the intersection of Liberty Street with Lowell Road. A left turn here leads back to Monument Square, a right turn up Lowell Road to Barrett's Mill Road.

Lowell Road

Although the structures along Lowell Road are mostly private homes, the visitor drawn by Concord's Colonial and Revolutionary history will want to travel it northward at least as far as Barrett's Mill Road, where several important landmarks are located. Lowell Road proceeds north, in the direction of Carlisle, from the Colonial Inn end of Monument Square, running from the left as the visitor faces the inn building. (To the extreme left, at 7 Lowell Road, directly across Lowell Road from the Colonial Inn, sits Concord's Christian Science Church.)

Peter Bulkeley Marker As part of its 1885 observances of the two hundred and fiftieth anniversary of its incorporation, the Town of Concord erected a number of markers at key historic sites. One of them—a bronze plate set in granite—was placed a short distance from where Lowell Road departs from Monument Square, on the right when heading north. This marker was intended to commemorate the house site of Peter Bulkeley (founder and first minister of Concord) and the spot where the land comprising Concord was sold to the English settlers by the local Native Americans. However, subsequent research has suggested that Bulkeley's house stood—and the bargain between the settlers, Squaw Sachem, Tahattawan, and others was struck—roughly at the corner where the Middlesex Hotel stood in the nineteenth century rather than at the location of this marker.

Old Calf Pasture Lying on the left side of Lowell Road on the way to Carlisle, a short distance beyond the Peter Bulkeley marker and just before the bridge across the Concord River, the Old Calf Pasture is now conservation land held and stewarded by the Town of Concord. In the seventeenth century, under Peter Bulkeley's ownership, this open meadowland served as pasturage. It later took on recreational importance, providing river frontage on which the Concord Canoe Club maintained a boathouse. Today, under the management of Concord's Division of Natural Resources, it offers opportunities for launching boats, picnicking, and enjoying the outdoors. (Boat rentals are commercially available at the South Bridge Boat House on Main Street.) The guidelines that pertain to use of the Calf Pasture are accessible on the Concord Department of Natural Resources Web pages, at http://www.concordma.gov/pages/ConcordMA_NaturalResources/ conservationland/consland.

Hunt's Bridge (Red Bridge) Concord's rivers—the Sudbury and the Assabet, which join at Egg Rock to form the Concord just a little upstream from the bridge at Lowell Road—were defining landscape features long before the first English settlers arrived in the 1630s. Musketaquid, Concord's Native American name, signified both the rivers and the surrounding grassy marshlands through which they flowed. The Indians used the rivers for transportation and food. The hay required by descendants of the English settlers to feed their cattle grew in the river meadows. Later, the rivers offered opportunities for recreation and reflection.

Because the rivers must be negotiated in getting about Concord (and especially because they are subject to seasonal flooding and to storm-related overflow), the town's bridges have quite a history of

Red Bridge, ca. 1892, from cabinet card by Alfred Munroe

building, repair, and replacement. Hunt's Bridge across the Concord River at Lowell Road is no exception. A bridge was first built on the spot in the late eighteenth century. In the nineteenth and early twentieth century, the wooden version of it then standing was descriptively called the Red Bridge. The Red Bridge was replaced in 1909 and its successor transferred to the state in 1945. When rebuilt in the 1960s, the Lowell Road bridge was renamed Hunt's Bridge after the early Concord family that owned property in its vicinity.

The visitor heading up Lowell Road comes to Hunt's Bridge not long after leaving Monument Square. In crossing it, look to the left to catch a glimpse of the confluence of the Sudbury and the Assabet at Egg Rock. One of the markers erected by the town in 1885 was placed at Egg Rock, where boaters can read the text on it today.

Hunt-Hosmer House and Barn   The Hunt-Hosmer House at 320 Lowell Road is situated on the right side of the road just beyond Hunt's Bridge. Although privately owned and not open to visitors, it is worth a look in passing because of important associations with Concord's early history and also with nineteenth-century author Henry David Thoreau.

The Hunt-Hosmer House was one of two houses constructed on the property it occupies by members of the Hunt family. The earlier of these was a seventeenth-century structure with an overhanging second story. Humphrey Hunt was the last of the family to own the older building, which was eventually taken down by farmer Edmund Hosmer.

Early Concord settler William Hunt bought and left his son Isaac a double house lot, which Isaac traded in 1669 to his brother Samuel for other property. In 1692, Samuel traded his Concord house and land to Adam Winthrop (grandson of Governor John Winthrop) for real estate elsewhere in Concord. In 1701, Winthrop left the former Hunt land to his son, from whom John Hunt (nephew of Isaac and Samuel) bought it back. The second house (the house that still stands) was built shortly after this—possibly in 1703—by John Hunt.

The property and houses passed from John Hunt to his son Simon in 1751, and from Simon to his son Reuben, father of Humphrey, who subsequently inherited them. Humphrey Hunt died in 1852, and Edmund Hosmer acquired the estate soon after. Hosmer, a farmer respected by Emerson and Thoreau, lived in the newer house and demolished the older building in 1859. Hosmer's friend Henry David Thoreau was fascinated by the old Humphrey Hunt place. He visited it repeatedly, and described the details of its architecture, construction, and—ultimately—destruction in several journal entries.

Now extensively renovated to serve residential purposes, the very large, English-style barn near the Hunt-Hosmer House until recently provided an impressive, intact example of eighteenth-century construction.

Hildreth's Corner and Barrett's Mill Road   About half a mile up Lowell Road beyond Hunt's Bridge, the visitor will come to a four-way stop, where Barrett's Mill Road leads off to the left. At the corner, at 8 Barrett's Mill Road, sits the handsome brick Jonathan Hildreth House (privately owned), the work in 1750 of architect and builder Reuben Duren, expanded in 1941 by owner Andrew Hepburn, an architect involved in the restoration at Colonial Williamsburg.

Heading down Barrett's Mill Road from Lowell Road, the visitor will pass the Abishai Brown House and Tavern ("Widow Brown's Tavern"; 71 Barrett's Mill) on the left. The widow of Abishai Brown kept a tavern in this building at the time of the Concord Fight, and British soldiers stopped here on the way back from searching the Barrett farm for military stores. (The right of dower, or "widow's thirds," assured a Colonial widow only of the use of a third of her deceased husband's real estate for life, and tavern-keeping was one of the few ways she might earn money to support herself.) The place was also home to Abishai Brown, Jr. (1746–1799), captain of one of Concord's two militia companies on April 19, 1775. Farther down the road, on the right, sits the Temple-Stone-Barrett-Merriam House (222 Barrett's Mill), where cabinet maker and pencil maker William Munroe—father of the founder of the Concord Free Public Library—lived with his family at two different periods during the first half of the nineteenth century.

Spencer Brook and Barrett's Mill Farther down on the right, at Spencer Brook (just before the intersection of Strawberry Hill Road with Barrett's Mill Road), the visitor will come to the site of a mill complex that served Concord from the seventeenth century into the twentieth. A gristmill was built on Spencer Brook in the seventeenth century. Around 1730, a sawmill was constructed next to it. Many of Concord's early houses were built or enlarged with lumber milled

Wagons at Hildreth's Corner, en route to Barrett's Mill, between 1900 and 1905

Barrett's Mill (grist mill) in winter,
early 20th century

on Spencer Brook. Later, the sawmill there turned out ties for the railroads that changed the economy and life of Concord in the nineteenth century.

During the eighteenth century and part of the nineteenth, the mills were owned and run by the Barrett family. They passed from Barrett ownership to Daniel Angier in the nineteenth century, and from Angier to Newton Gross about 1890. Gross ran both mills until 1918, and later sold them to George A. Baker, from whom they passed to John Forbes.

By 1920, people had started to buy ready-ground flour and meal in stores. The demand for the gristmill on Barrett's Mill Road declined sharply, and it fell into decay. The sawmill had a longer life, remaining in use into the 1950s.

Colonel James Barrett Farm The Barrett Farm at 448 Barrett's Mill Road is key to the story of the Concord Fight. On April 19, 1775, Colonel James Barrett—who then occupied this house—commanded a regiment of militia and all Colonial troops present in Concord. He was also in charge of the supplies and ammunition that the Provincial Congress had ordered stored in Concord in the event that conflict with British troops made such forethought necessary, and his own home was one of the storehouses. Despite the colonists' attempt to maintain secrecy about the storage of supplies, British leaders had their informants. The British military commanders who marched on Concord on April 19, 1775, were well aware of Barrett's central role and that his home was among those where stores were hidden. Under Barrett's supervision, some stores were moved out of Concord or more carefully hidden when it became clear that the British were on their way. Nevertheless, bullets, flints, cartridges, cannon, and cannon carriages remained on the property.

On the morning of April 19, Captain Lawrence Parsons led several companies of British light infantry over the North Bridge to the Barrett farmhouse, but was largely thwarted in his mission of seizing and destroying stores. Most of the concealed ammunition and supplies had by then been moved elsewhere, and the haste of the British search worked against discovery of what was left. Parsons and his men returned to the North Bridge after the exchange of gunfire there was over.

Built by Colonel Barrett's father in 1705, the old farmhouse remained in Barrett family hands until 1894, later passing to the McGrath family. Although the surrounding fields were continuously farmed, over time the house fell into disrepair. Late in 2003, the preservation organization Save Our Heritage purchased some of the property surrounding it, acquiring the house itself and the remaining property two years later with the intention of restoration and ultimate transfer to Minute Man National Historical Park. The stabilization of the house and its renovation were accomplished through private donations and grant funding. In April 2009, President Barack Obama signed legislation extending the boundary of Minute Man National Historical Park to include Barrett's Farm, paving the way for incorporating the property into the park (realized in 2012).

The Barrett Farm is on the National Register of Historic Places and in Concord's Barrett Farm Historic District. It is currently open to the public on a limited basis. Additional details about the house are accessible on the Barrett Farm pages at http://jamesbarrettfarm.org.

Colonel James Barrett Farm, 1890s, from cabinet card by Alfred Winslow Hosmer

Having retraced their footsteps along Barrett's Mill Road back to Lowell Road, visitors may return to the center of Concord by taking a right at the intersection of Barrett's Mill and Lowell Roads, and following Lowell Road to Monument Square.

The Estabrook Woods—An Excursion into Thoreau Country
There is hardly an inch of Concord that author and naturalist Henry David Thoreau did not know intimately. The Estabrook Woods, in the northwest part of Concord, was among the places where Thoreau loved to walk. He wrote in his journal on June 10, 1853, for example:

> *What shall this great wild tract over which we strolled be called— Many farmers have pastures there & wood lots—& orchards— It consists mainly of rocky pastures— It contains what I call the Boulder Field—the Yellow Birch swamp—The Black-Birch Hill—the Laurel Pasture—The Hog Pasture—The White Pine Grove—The Eastebrooks Place—The Old Lime-Kiln—the Lime Quarries—Spruce swamp The Ermine Weazel Woods— Also the Oak Meadowss [sic]— the Cedar Swamp—The Kibbe Place—& the Old Place N W of Brooks Clarks— Ponkawtasset bounds it on the S. There are a few frog ponds & an old mill pond within it & Bateman's Pond on its edge . . . The Old Carlisle Road which runs through the middle of it is bordered on each side with wild apple pastures . . . It is a paradise for walkers in the fall.*

Thoreau's father ran a sawmill in Estabrook to cut cedar for use in making pencils.

Visitors inspired by the life and writings of this literary son of Concord may want to explore the Estabrook Woods. Most of Estabrook Country is privately owned, a good deal of it by Harvard University's Museum of Comparative Zoology. Some is held by the nearby Middlesex School, and some is under municipal or land trust ownership. Public access to most of the area is allowed. A sight-seeing detour through the Estabrook Woods can occupy hours, so Thoreauvians should plan to undertake it when there is ample time for the purpose.

To reach Estabrook from Concord Center, take Lowell Road in the direction of Barrett's Mill Road. At Hildreth's Corner, take a right onto Barnes Hill Road. (Across Lowell Road, Barrett's Mill Road becomes Barnes Hill Road.) Just before the North Bridge Visitor Center of Minute Man National Historical Park, take a left from Barnes Hill Road onto Estabrook Road and proceed until the pavement ends. There is a small parking area here which visitors may use. If touring Estabrook after taking in the sights of Barrett's Mill Road, simply follow Barrett's Mill back to Lowell Road, cross Lowell onto Barnes Hill, and turn left off Barnes Hill Road onto Estabrook.

It is still possible to walk the dirt road through Estabrook all the way up to the neighboring town of Carlisle, but visitors should bear in mind that spring and fall rains, flooding, and winter ice and snow make for poor footing. Sturdy footwear is essential in any season, and insect repellent is useful. Moreover, the trails in Estabrook are unmarked, so it is advisable to carry a map of the area.

Those interested in researching the rich history of this area might wish to precede a walk through Estabrook with a visit to the archives of the Concord Free Public Library, which holds considerable research material on the subject. For hours and contact information, visit the library website (http://www.concordlibrary.org).

Bedford Street

Surveyed by Henry David Thoreau in the 1850s, Bedford Street—so named because it runs toward the neighboring town of Bedford—now forms a segment of Route 62, a Massachusetts state highway. Bedford Street starts at Monument Square, between the Town House (22 Monument Square) and the Holy Family Church (12 Monument Square).

Dee Funeral Home Located on the left side of the street a short distance from the Square, Dee's Funeral Home (27 Bedford Street) is an active private business which, because of its long history in Concord, merits mention, even though it's not a tourist stop. In the nineteenth century, the Dees worked for Willard Farrar, Concord's first burial agent, ultimately taking over the Farrar funeral business, which

View down Bedford Street toward Sleepy Hollow Cemetery, ca. 1890,
by Alfred Winslow Hosmer

generations of the family have since continued. The Dees still own the horse-drawn town hearse that carried Ralph Waldo Emerson to his final resting place in Sleepy Hollow Cemetery in 1882, and was later used for the 2006 reinterment ceremonies for Sophia and Una Hawthorne (Nathaniel Hawthorne's wife and older daughter), who were originally buried in England.

Just beyond the complex of Dee-owned buildings, the visitor will reach an intersection where Bedford Street continues to the right. Diagonally across the road from the intersection, at 24 Court Lane, sits the former mortuary chapel and hearse house for Sleepy Hollow Cemetery. This building—which originally served as the North Center Schoolhouse and was converted to funerary purposes several decades after Sleepy Hollow opened—now serves as office space for Concord's Assessing Department.

Sleepy Hollow Cemetery   Sleepy Hollow Cemetery was formally dedicated in 1855. It incorporates areas opened in 1823 and 1855, and another section opened in the 1860s (the old Middlesex Agricultural fairground, located between the 1823 and 1855 sections). "The Knoll," a new section with an area consecrated for Jewish burials, was opened in 1998.

The New Burying Ground (or New Hill Burying Ground)—predecessor and, since 1855, part of Sleepy Hollow Cemetery—is adjacent to the old mortuary chapel at 24 Court Lane. By 1823, when it was opened, the old Hill Burying Ground and South Burying Ground had reached capacity. Anna Robbins was the first person buried in the new cemetery. Members of the Thoreau family (including author Henry David Thoreau) were originally buried in the 1823 cemetery and later moved to Authors' Ridge in Sleepy Hollow. Martha Hunt, the nineteen-year-old suicide whose wrenching story Nathaniel Hawthorne captured in his journal and later drew upon in describing the search for Zenobia's body in *The Blithedale Romance,* was buried here in 1845.

Laid out on land purchased from the estate of Deacon Reuben Brown, Sleepy Hollow was named—according to George Bradford Bartlett in his 1880 *Concord Guide Book*—for the natural "amphitheatre" that "had borne the name of Sleepy Hollow long before it was thought of as a burial place." The choice of name may or may not also have reflected local familiarity with Washington Irving's "The Legend of Sleepy Hollow" (published in 1820 in Irving's *Sketch Book*). In any event, before it was transformed into a cemetery, the area attracted walkers and those seeking a tranquil spot to rest and refresh themselves.

Sleepy Hollow Cemetery, late 19th century

The 1855 section of Sleepy Hollow Cemetery was laid out according to plans drawn by landscape design partners Horace William Shaler Cleveland and Robert Morris Copeland. Ralph Waldo Emerson delivered the keynote address at its dedication on September 29, 1855. The expanded cemetery was planned with an eye to tranquility and private contemplation. Cleveland and Copeland avoided the imposition of a geometric grid of lots over the terrain, preferring to place them on paths that followed the natural outlines of the land, and respecting native trees and plants. Their sense of landscape design was in harmony with Emerson's Transcendental approach to aesthetics. In his Sleepy Hollow dedication speech, Emerson extolled the natural landscape as the proper focus of the landscape architect: "Modern taste has shown that there is no ornament, no architecture alone, so sumptuous as well disposed woods and waters, where art has been employed only to remove superfluities, and bring out the natural advantages."

Today, Sleepy Hollow—sometimes called "America's Westminster Abbey" because of the remarkable number of distinguished people laid to rest in it—is a tourist destination for thousands of

Thoreau grave markers in Sleepy Hollow Cemetery, 1890s,
by Alfred Winslow Hosmer

pilgrims to Concord annually. It is
listed on the National Register of
Historic Places. There are several
Bedford Street entrances to the cemetery, including the central Prichard
Gate, built in 1891 and rebuilt in
1947. Visitors who drive into Sleepy
Hollow may park in a small lot at
the foot of Authors' Ridge.

Many come to Sleepy Hollow
specifically to honor Emerson's memory by his grave in the Emerson family plot on Authors' Ridge (located
on the far side of the large Hollow,
to the left, as one approaches from
Bedford Street). Emerson's grave marker of rose quartz bears lines from his
poem "The Problem." In addition
to Emerson and Thoreau, Concord
authors Nathaniel Hawthorne, Bronson Alcott, Louisa May Alcott, and

*Wood path in Sleepy Hollow
Cemetery, 1890s, by Alfred
Winslow Hosmer*

Margaret Sidney (pseudonym for Harriett Mulford Stone—or Mrs.
Daniel Lothrop—who wrote the "Five Little Pepper" series for children)
are buried on Author's Ridge, as are members of the locally prominent
Keyes, Brooks, and Wheeler families.

But there is more to see in Sleepy Hollow Cemetery than the
graves of Concord's literary luminaries on the ridge. To aid navigation
of the cemetery's considerable acreage, a map is available for purchase
at the Concord Visitor Center (58 Main Street) and also in the Town
House (22 Monument Square).

Entering by the Prichard Gate, the visitor quickly comes to a
fork, the left branch of which leads to sculptor Daniel Chester French's
Mourning Victory, also known as the Melvin Memorial. This marble piece was commissioned by James Melvin, a Civil War veteran,
in memory of his brothers Asa, John, and Samuel (Concord boys
who died in the conflict) and dedicated in 1909. French—a friend
of James Melvin—was also the sculptor of the *Minute Man* at the

North Bridge and the seated Lincoln in the Lincoln Memorial in Washington.

Returning along the path that leads to the Melvin Memorial, the right branch of the fork will take the visitor to the Hollow, a natural kettle hole containing many gravesites. In the Hollow and on the rises along its perimeter are buried many whose names are familiar, including Transcendentalist, educator, and social reformer Elizabeth Palmer Peabody; the Hoar family, whose plot includes the graves of Samuel Hoar, the nineteenth-century founder of a dynasty of powerful lawyers, his daughter Elizabeth Hoar (a learned woman and an intimate of the Emerson family), and her brothers, Judge Ebenezer Rockwood Hoar (Attorney General of the United States under President Ulysses S. Grant) and United States Senator George Frisbie Hoar; schoolmaster and abolitionist Frank Sanborn, one of the "Secret Six" who funded and helped to arm John Brown prior to his raid on Harpers Ferry, Virginia (now West Virginia); Ephraim Wales Bull, who developed the Concord Grape; and sculptor Daniel Chester French (whose grave is located on the elevated path to the left of the Hollow when approaching Author's Ridge from the direction of Bedford Street).

Those who grow weary of the burial places of eminent people might seek out the grave of Sheila Shea, who died in 1986. The irreverent, controversial, and surprisingly well known inscription on her marker reads, "Who the hell is Sheila Shea?"

Sleepy Hollow Cemetery contains more than ten thousand gravesites. Parts of it are still in active use. Like all of Concord's cemeteries, it is open from 7:00 A.M. until dusk or 8:00 P.M., whichever comes earlier, weather permitting. Regulations pertaining to Concord's cemeteries are accessible on the Town of Concord's website (http://www.concord ma.gov). Genealogists who want to confirm whether someone is buried in Sleepy Hollow should contact the office of the Concord Town Clerk ((978) 318-3080; or, by e-mail, TownClerk@concordma.gov).

Great Meadows National Wildlife Refuge   Birders and others who enjoy the out-of-doors will want to visit the Great Meadows National Wildlife Refuge, which is operated by the United States Fish and Wildlife Service. For centuries, these meadows provided the hay that fed local livestock. Former slaves Caesar Robbins and

Jack Garrison once lived on Concord's Great Meadows. Naturalist Henry David Thoreau and ornithologist William Brewster closely observed the abundant wildlife here. In 1944, lawyer, outdoorsman, and Concord resident Samuel Hoar (great-grandson of Squire Sam Hoar) donated to the federal government multiple parcels of meadowland on the Concord River, forming what would become the nucleus of the refuge. As a hunter and an observer of wildlife, Hoar loved the Great Meadows. He devoted considerable thought and energy to enhancing the meadows as a "stopover" for migrating birds, and over the years bought up parcels from multiple landowners. His gift to the government was expanded by subsequent acquisitions, extending the refuge beyond Concord into Bedford, Billerica, Carlisle, Lincoln, Sudbury, and Wayland.

The Sudbury Unit of Great Meadows (including office and visitor center) is located at 73 Weir Hill Road (phone number (978) 443-4661). The Concord Unit, open to the public from sunrise to sunset, is located on Monsen Road. To reach it, continue up Bedford Street (Route 62) for a mile or so beyond Sleepy Hollow Cemetery, and take a left onto Monsen. The Concord parking lot for Great Meadows is about half a mile down the road. Bathroom facilities are available for visitors. Information about the refuge is accessible on the Great Meadows website, at http://www.fws.gov/refuge/great_meadows/.

Daniel Chester French in Great Meadows, 1890s, by Alfred Winslow Hosmer

Main Street

Back at Monument Square, the visitor may explore the business district of Concord Center (known locally as the Mill Dam) and then
continue on to several key locations down Main Street. The section
of Main Street through the center of town is the successor to a seventeenth-century road off the Common. Before English settlement of
the town, the Native Americans maintained a fishing weir on the Mill
Brook. The brook, which now runs under Main Street, was dammed
to provide power for the gristmill built by Concord founder and minister Peter Bulkeley. The damming of the Mill Brook created a mill
pond between the present Walden Street and Lexington Road, from
Heywood Street to Main.

The early version of what is now Main Street curved and wound
about a good deal more than does the modern road. In the seventeenth
century, it ran on the east, north, and west sides of the South Burying
Ground rather than on the south side, as it does today. Main Street—
part of Route 62—now crosses Route 2, passes through West Concord
(which is part of Concord proper—not a separate town), and runs all
the way to the Acton line.

Concord Center, south side of Main Street, looking west, ca. 1865

While Main Street in Concord Center dates as far back as English settlement, the majority of buildings along it were built well after the Colonial period. Beginning in the mid-1820s, the Mill Dam area was completely overhauled by the Concord Mill Dam Company, a real estate development corporation. The company bought up property in the center of Concord, drained the mill pond, tore down some buildings, renovated others, and put up new structures that were offered for sale or rent. On the north side of Main Street, the innovations of the Mill Dam Company included the pillared Concord Bank and Middlesex Mutual Fire Insurance Company building at 46 Main Street (now a shoe store). Next to the bank (one building closer to Monument Square), the present 42-44 Main Street (now Main Street's Market & Café) was constructed on the site of Peter Bulkeley's seventeenth-century mill. (Indeed, the face of the Mill Dam as it looked in the mid-nineteenth century survives today much as it was when Emerson, Thoreau, and the Alcotts knew it.) Nearby on the north side of the street, at 58 Main Street, the Concord Visitor Center (http://www.concordchamberofcommerce.org/visitor-information/) provides a good place for planning an itinerary or researching local amenities and services.

South Burying Ground Just a little beyond the Visitor Center, on the same side of the street but farther west (across Keyes Road), is located the South Burying Ground, the newer of Concord's two seventeenth-century cemeteries (the older being the Hill Burying Ground off Monument Square). Called the South Burying Ground in the Concord town records, it is now often referred to as the Main Street Burying Ground. It has also occasionally been called the Smedley Burying Ground, because in the seventeenth century it was situated adjacent to the property of James Smedley. Although it has been suggested that the land on which the South Burying Ground is located was private property before conversion to town use, the lack of any record of transfer supports the likelihood that it was from the beginning held in common by inhabitants of the town.

There are no records pinpointing exactly when the South Burying Ground was established. The earliest grave marker here is that of Thomas Hartshorn, who died in 1697. Like the Hill, the South

*South Burying Ground on
Main Street, before 1930,
when the house in the photograph
(the Block House) was moved
to Lowell Road*

Burying Ground was used for decades before the installment of the earliest surviving stone in it. This is apparently why the descendants of Nathaniel Billings, who died in 1673 but for whom there is no original stone in the cemetery, placed a commemorative marker for him here, among Billings family gravestones. Be that as it may, between 1697 and the last burial in 1855 (the year Sleepy Hollow Cemetery was dedicated), some two hundred and thirty stones were erected in the South Burying Ground. Among the Concordians buried here are Revolutionary War veterans and one minister of the First Parish.

Why did early Concordians feel the need for two cemeteries within a stone's throw of each other? The answer is unclear. Perhaps after several decades of using the Hill, they felt that space was getting tight there. Or the gradual settlement of areas beyond the town center may have created demand for a second cemetery to accommodate residents of the South Quarter and the western part of town. Certainly, the South Burying Ground serves as the final resting place for a number of South Quarter families, Billings, Buss, Dakin, Hubbard, Lee, Miles, Potter, and Shevalley among them. A few local historians have suggested that Colonial superstition against carrying a body over running water played a role. From a strictly practical point of view, the condition of the Mill Dam and the difficulty of hauling heavy coffins across it are more likely to have been factors.

Like the Hill Burying Ground and Sleepy Hollow Cemetery, the South Burying Ground is open from 7:00 A.M. to 8:00 P.M. or dusk, whichever comes earlier, weather permitting. Rubbings are not allowed. Researchers may consult a grave listing and map in the Special Collections of the Concord Free Public Library to locate specific graves.

Grave markers of Hannah and Ephraim Brown, South Burying Ground,
mid-20th century photograph

Concord Free Public Library Continuing west on Main Street from
the South Burying Ground, the visitor soon comes to the intersection of Main Street and Sudbury Road, where, at the official address
129 Main Street, stands the Concord Free Public Library—a research
facility for a local, regional, national, and international clientele, and
a much-loved institution.

Dedicated on October 1, 1873, the Concord Free Public Library
was founded through the generosity and vision of William Munroe, a
Concord native who made a fortune in dry goods and textiles and after
retirement developed a desire to use his accumulated wealth to benefit
the town where he had been born and raised. Munroe provided funds
to construct the library building, masterminded the details of construction and operation, and formed the Concord Free Public Library
Corporation to oversee the buildings, grounds, and valuable holdings.
The institution he established was and remains an amalgam of public
and private funding and management. The original Victorian Gothic
building (built on the site of the home of Nathan and Mary Merrick

Lending Department [Concord Free Public Library],
from mounted print by A. H. Folsom, 1873

Brooks, which was moved to Hubbard Street to permit construction
of the library) has been much-renovated and enlarged since 1873, but
survives as the lobby of the current building. Munroe hired the Boston
architectural firm of Snell and Gregerson to design his library. A major renovation and expansion under Frohman, Robb, & Little in the
1930s altered the façade dramatically from Gothic to Georgian.

   Within a decade of its establishment, the Concord Free Public
Library became a local landmark, a must-see for visitors to the town,
and a recognized temple of New England culture. Whether or not they
have a research mission, visitors are welcome to stop by the library
today. The building is impressive in and of itself. Moreover, there is a
good selection of Concord-related art displayed for the enjoyment of
all—in the lobby, Reference Room, Thoreau Room, Trustees' Room,
Special Collections Reading Room, and elsewhere—with interpretive
signage to enrich a self-paced tour. The library holds major works of
art—portraits and busts of Concord luminaries, sculptures by Daniel
Chester French, Louisa Lander, Walton Ricketson, Frank Edwin Elwell,
Anna Hyatt Huntington, and Mary Ogden Abbott, and paintings by
Washington Allston, David Scott, William James Stillman, May Alcott

(youngest sister of author Louisa May Alcott), Stacy Tolman, Elizabeth Wentworth Roberts, Edward Emerson Simmons, and N. C. Wyeth. Daniel Chester French's large marble sculpture of Emerson (seated) dominates the library lobby and imbues the place with a Transcendental aura.

Named in honor of the library's founder, the **William Munroe Special Collections** comprise the most comprehensive archive of primary and secondary source material relating to Concord history, life, landscape, literature, people, and influence from 1635 to the present day. Researchers may use the Special Collections during regularly scheduled hours. Appointments are not required except to view photographic holdings. The department's staff can often accommodate casual visitors—aficionados of Emerson or Thoreau or Louisa May Alcott who hope to see first editions or manuscripts but who have no specific research purpose—without a prior appointment. Once a year (and occasionally more), the department offers a major gallery exhibition on a Concord-related topic. These displays are free and open to the public.

Special Collections holdings document the history and literature of Concord, and also local residents, events, institutions, and organizations. Printed books, archival and manuscript materials, pamphlets, ephemera, broadsides, maps, photographic and pictorial holdings, municipal records, printed town reports, street directories, vital records,

Just-renovated Concord Free Public Library, 1934

genealogical volumes, historic building files, works of art, artifacts, and other types of material may all be used by the researcher here. Online cataloging records of holdings are available through the Minuteman Library Network and (nationally) through OCLC.

The Concord Free Public Library homepage at www.concord library.org provides access to a great deal of information about the library—hours, phone numbers, staff e-mail addresses, holdings, governance, policies, data base and museum pass availability, programs and events, and more—and, on the Special Collections pages, extensive historical context drawing upon and showcasing materials in the Special Collections. A virtual visit to the library website is valuable in preparation for a visit to the library itself. Class groups should contact Special Collections staff directly at (978) 318-3342 to schedule on-site presentations of archival holdings or to arrange for group projects.

One Saturday each June, the Friends of the Concord Free Public Library hold a major book sale on the library's front lawn. The visitor fortunate enough to be in town then won't want to miss this event. Check the library's website before your trip to Concord to find out whether your planned visit will coincide with the sale.

Main Street near Concord Free Public Library, looking west, 1870s, from card stereograph

*Residence of Judge Hoar with President Grant (second from left) and cabinet,
who were in town for the centennial celebration of the Concord Fight, 1875*

Main Street Beyond the Library The section of Main Street running west from the library was once lined with graceful elm trees. Although the elms are long gone, this neighborhood maintains a great
deal of architectural integrity. From the intersection of Main Street
and Sudbury Road (where the library sits), a walk west down Main
Street (the road to the right, when facing the front of the library) will
take the visitor past a number of historic houses. Some of these buildings are owned by Concord Academy, a well-known boarding and day
school. Examples include the Samuel Hoar House (Concord Academy's
Admadjaja House) at 158 Main Street, where the first in a line of famous
Concord lawyers lived; the Josiah Davis Double House (the Academy's
Aloian House) at 166 Main Street, in the nineteenth century a rental
property occupied by a succession of tenants, among them Lemuel
Shattuck (author of the first full-scale history of Concord) and the John
Thoreau family (when David Henry—later known as Henry David—
was a boy); and the Ebenezer Rockwood Hoar House (the Academy's
Hobson House) at 194 Main Street, the home of one of Squire Sam's
sons, a lawyer and judge who served as United States Attorney General
under President Grant.

Antislavery/Underground Railroad Sites   The William Whiting House at 169 Main Street once formed part of a nexus of antislavery and Underground Railroad households, beginning where the Concord Free Public Library now stands and proceeding west along both Main Street and Sudbury Road. Antislavery leader Mary Merrick Brooks lived in the house that was originally located on the library site and today stands at 45 Hubbard Street. Involved in organized antislavery at the local, county, and state levels, Colonel William Whiting was Mrs. Brooks's close colleague. Just across the street from the Brooks house, in what is now 19 Sudbury Road, blacksmith Francis Edwin Bigelow and his wife Ann harbored fugitive slave Shadrach Minkins in mid-February 1851. Schoolmaster Frank Sanborn, an activist toward keeping the territory of Kansas free and one of the so-called "Secret Six" who raised funds for radical abolitionist Captain John Brown, lived and taught at 49 Sudbury. (His students included the Emerson children, Julian Hawthorne, and two daughters of John Brown.) Early in April 1860 (four months after Brown was executed), federal deputies attempted to arrest Sanborn here for supporting Brown in his plans for an armed slave uprising and his 1859 raid on the arsenal at Harpers Ferry, Virginia (now West Virginia). Others in the Main Street/Sudbury Road triangle—the Hoars and Thoreaus included—were also committed abolitionists. The Thoreaus attended antislavery conventions and signed their names to petitions calling for radical measures, opened their home to prominent abolitionists visiting Concord, and provided lodging and aid to free blacks and fugitive slaves (for example, to Henry Williams of Virginia in 1851).

Thoreau-Alcott House   Visitors to Concord—and especially to the Concord Free Public Library—frequently inquire about the street address of the house where Henry David Thoreau died. The Thoreau-Alcott House at 255 Main Street—associated not only with Thoreau but also with Concord authors Amos Bronson Alcott and Louisa May Alcott—remains under private ownership today. Although it's impossible to visit and tour it, there is nothing to prevent the literary pilgrim from stopping for a moment on the sidewalk in front to pay quiet homage.

In September of 1849, Henry Thoreau's father John purchased the Main Street house, known at the time as the "Yellow House." He undertook renovations to it and in August of 1850 moved his family into it from his "Texas House" (no longer standing) on Belknap Street in Concord. The Thoreaus maintained their pencil business in the Yellow House, but eventually left behind the manufacture of pencils for the production of ground lead for electrotyping. Henry Thoreau surveyed the Yellow House lot in May of 1850. During his family's residence here, his room was the finished third-floor attic, which was spacious enough to accommodate his books, arrowheads, rocks, birds' eggs, and botanical collections. He died in the Yellow House in May of 1862.

Thoreau-Alcott House, ca. 1905, by Henry Allen Castle

Although other Concord residences more readily come to mind in connection with the Alcott family (particularly The Wayside and Orchard House on Lexington Road), the Yellow House was the final Concord home of Bronson and Louisa May Alcott. Having achieved financial security through the success of *Little Women* and her subsequent children's books, Louisa Alcott provided more than half of the sum necessary to purchase the house. Her widowed sister Anna Pratt, her nephews, and her parents moved into it in November of 1877. (Louisa herself had a Boston residence by that time, and therefore stayed in the Yellow House only itermittently.) Abigail May Alcott (Abba)—mother of the Alcott girls and the model for "Marmee" in *Little Women*—died shortly after the move here.

Nashawtuc Hill A little farther west down Main Street, there is a traffic light at the intersection of Main Street, Thoreau Street (on the left), and Nashawtuc Road (on the right). Those interested in Concord's seventeenth-century history may wish to sidetrack off Main Street to the Nashawtuc Road bridge, which crosses the Sudbury River on the way to Nashawtuc Hill. Nashawtuc, meaning "between the rivers," is the Native American name for the hill commonly called Lee's Hill in Thoreau's time. Looking to the right from the bridge while approaching Nashawtuc Hill, on the far side of the river the visitor will see the site of the former Willard-Lee Farm. Originally the property of Simon Willard (who, along with Peter Bulkeley, was one of the founders of Concord), the farm later belonged to Henry Woodis, during the Revolution to British sympathizer Joseph Lee, in the nineteenth century to Joseph Barrett and subsequently to David Elwell, for whom Thoreau surveyed it. The original farmhouse—altered and expanded over the years—burned in February 1857. In the late nineteenth and early twentieth century, prominent civil engineer William Wheeler made his home on Nashawtuc.

Elm Street and Sanborn House   Continuing west on Main Street past the intersection of Main, Thoreau, and Nashawtuc, the traveler quickly comes to a fork. Main Street continues to the left. To the right, Elm Street beckons those drawn by the history of nineteenth-century New England roads and by Concord's literary and reform history.

Elm Street was laid out late in the first decade of the nineteenth century as the eastern end of the Union Turnpike. Constructed to connect the Cambridge and Concord Turnpike and the terminus of the Fifth Massachusetts Turnpike in Leominster, the Union Turnpike formed part of a complex web of toll roads that crossed Massachusetts, anticipating the railroad and (much later) Route 2 in linking the state's towns and cities. The construction of turnpike roads flourished in New England from around 1790 until the mid-nineteenth century. Their management provides a prime example of public/private collaboration. State legislatures granted private turnpike corporations like the Union Turnpike Corporation (founded in 1804) the right to build and operate roads on which tolls were collected at tollgates. In return for providing private funding for and long-term maintenance of what was essentially a public improvement, the corporation could keep the tolls collected at its tollgates. If the road was well-traveled, stockholders in the corporation profited. But the Union Turnpike did not attract heavy traffic. It became a public road in 1829 (in Worcester County) and 1830 (in Middlesex County). Its beginning section in Concord was officially named Elm Street in 1854.

Heading away from Concord Center on Elm Street, students of nineteenth-century Concord will find the Franklin Sanborn House (still a residence) on the right, at 106 Elm, just before the bridge over the Sudbury River. A private schoolmaster and an ardent abolitionist, Frank Sanborn was also a journalist, newspaper editor, secretary of the Massachusetts State Board of Charities, and a prolific biographer and editor of Concord's Transcendental authors. Having lived in several Concord locations, he built this house on Elm Street in 1880. For a decade preceding the death of poet William Ellery Channing in 1901, Channing—a particular friend of Henry David Thoreau—lived here as Sanborn's guest.

South Bridge Boat House From the Sanborn House, Main Street is regained by backtracking toward the intersection of Main and Elm, taking a right onto River Street (before the Elm/Main intersection), and then a right onto Main. The South Bridge Boat House on the Sudbury River is located at 496 Main Street, a short distance west from River Street. Constructed in the 1890s as the boathouse for the Concord Home School, it was converted to commercial use in the twentieth century. Built at a time when a number of private recreational boathouses were maintained by individuals, families, clubs, and groups, this boathouse now accommodates much of the boating activity on Concord's rivers. Purchased in 1949 by George and Shirley Rohan, the South Bridge Boat House offers canoe and kayak rentals for hearty explorers who want to investigate

South Bridge Boat House, 1890s, when owned by the Concord Home School

the Sudbury, Assabet, and Concord Rivers on their own, and (by reservation) tea, lunch, and dinner cruises for visitors to enjoy while they take in the riverscape. Additional information may be obtained on the boathouse website (www.southbridgeboathouse.com) or by calling (978) 369-9438 or (978) 371-1785 regarding cruises and catering.

Joseph Hosmer House and "The Dovecote" The Joseph Hosmer House at 572 Main Street and the Hosmer Cottage at 586 Main Street—both private residences—are located a little beyond the South Bridge Boat House, just past the railroad bridge over Main Street, on the right side of the street when approaching West Concord. Joseph Hosmer occupied the house at 572 Main—one of the oldest structures in Concord—in the eighteenth and early nineteenth centuries. A skilled cabinet maker and a farmer, he was also one of the Revolutionary heroes of April 19, 1775— the Colonial adjutant at the North Bridge and the man who, when smoke was observed coming from the town center, asked his comrades if they would allow the British to burn the town down. The Hosmer Cottage (just beyond the Joseph Hosmer House) is historically significant as the home of Amos Bronson Alcott and his growing family from 1840 to 1843. Youngest daughter May Alcott— later an artist—was born here in July of 1840. Louisa May Alcott later modeled her character Meg's honeymoon home "The Dovecote" in *Little Women* after the place.

West Concord Although tourists don't usually come to Concord specifically to see West Concord, this part of town is integral to Concord's local history, particularly its agricultural, manufacturing, and ethnic history. West Concord residents are keenly aware of the area's rich past and display a strong sense of neighborhood pride. The visitor with time to spare and a car or bicycle (check the area phone listings for bicycle rentals) might well choose to continue west on Main Street (Route 62) across Route 2 and into the downtown district of West Concord, which features a number of locally-owned stores, shops, and eateries. Two regionally well-known West Concord bakeries—Concord Teacakes and the Nashoba Brook Bakery—offer coffee, wonderful baked goods, and light fare.

To reach the business district of West Concord, take Commonwealth Avenue (the road to the right at the traffic light located at the Main Street/Commonwealth Avenue intersection). A short distance from the intersection, Commonwealth Avenue heads to the right, across gated railroad tracks.

Built in the 1890s, **Union Station**—the West Concord train depot at 20 Commonwealth Avenue—is listed on the National Register of Historic Places. Now part of the Commuter Rail system of the Massachusetts Bay Transportation Authority (MBTA), it is a significant artifact of Concord's railroad history. The Fitchburg Railroad came through Concord in 1844, bringing social, economic, commercial, and agricultural change with it. It opened in Concord Center first, later in West Concord. Concord's railroad connections expanded dramatically during the 1870s. In 1872, the Framingham and Lowell line intersected the Fitchburg line in West Concord, creating Concord Junction. In 1873, the Nashua, Acton, and Boston line also intersected the Fitchburg line at the Junction. Although Concord Junction was a beehive of railroad activity for decades, the rise of automobile travel, the development of the road system, and (eventually) the introduction of air travel in the twentieth century ultimately led to its decline. Nevertheless, the West Concord stop remains actively busy with commuters to Cambridge and Boston.

Visitors seeking computer access or a place to read and rest may wish to stop at the **Loring N. Fowler Memorial Library**—a branch of the Concord Free Public Library—at 1322 Main Street. Separated by some distance from the main library in Concord Center, the citizens of West Concord petitioned for a branch in 1918. In 1919, the West Concord Branch opened in one room of the West Concord Grammar School. In 1928, through the bequest of local merchant Loring N. Fowler, the construction of a separate branch building was undertaken. Designed by architect and Concord resident Harry Little of the Boston and Washington firm of Frohman, Robb & Little, the Loring N. Fowler Memorial Library was dedicated in 1930. A major renovation of the Colonial Revival building was completed in 1996; another was undertaken in 2010.

Those interested in Concord's role during the Civil War will find it worthwhile to travel about a mile farther west down Main Street from the intersection of Main and Commonwealth Avenue to glimpse the former **Damon Mill,** which has been converted to office space and now goes by the name Damonmill Square, with its official address on Pond Lane. Under the ownership of Edward Carver Damon, the mill produced cloth for Union Army uniforms.

As of this writing, a rail trail running from Lowell to Framingham is under construction. The **Bruce Freeman Rail Trail** will extend from Acton through West Concord to the neighboring town of Sudbury, following the old New Haven Railroad Framingham & Lowell line. The rail trail will provide opportunity for non-motorized recreational activities (walking, bicycling, jogging, snowshoeing, and cross-country skiing) and will allow pleasant travel between points of interest to visitors. For more information about the project, visit the Bruce Freeman Rail Trail website at http://www.brucefreemanrailtrail.org.

Thoreau Street and Concord Depot Heading back from West Concord across Route 2 to Concord Center via Main Street, the railroad enthusiast will find Concord's other depot by taking a right from Main Street onto Thoreau Street (at the traffic light at Main, Nashawtuc, and Thoreau). The Concord (or Fitchburg) Depot is located at 80-86 Thoreau Street, on the right side of the street when approached from Main. Occupied today by stores and businesses, the building is a late nineteenth-century successor to the original one constructed when the Fitchburg Railroad came to Concord in 1844. Sightseers who need public transportation in the direction of Boston (to the east) or Fitchburg (to the west) will find the waiting area for trains in either direction behind the depot building. Commuter Rail trains stop both in Concord Center and West Concord. Schedules and ticket purchase information relating to Commuter Rail trains are available on the MBTA website, at http://www.mbta.com/schedules_and_maps/rail/lines/?route=FITCHBRG.

Nine Acre Corner In good weather, those with ample time and a car or bicycle may enjoy a leisurely detour off the beaten tourist track to Nine Acre Corner, one of Concord's historically significant agricultural areas, still farmed today. To reach Nine Acre Corner from Thoreau

Street, continue a short distance along Thoreau from the Concord Depot to the intersection of Thoreau and Sudbury Road. Heeding the traffic signal here, turn right onto Sudbury, cross over the railroad tracks,
and continue on to Route 2, where there is another set of lights. Crossing the highway, stay on Sudbury Road over Heath's Bridge (across
the Sudbury River) all the way to Nine Acre Corner, at the intersection
of Sudbury and Route 117 (the Fitchburg Turnpike). Wheeler Road is
located to the right just before this intersection. The Verrill Farm farm
stand at Sudbury and Wheeler offers fresh produce and baked goods
and unhindered views of the surrounding fields. In the late nineteenth
and early twentieth centuries, when Concord was at the forefront of
hothouse gardening, successful farmer Frank Wheeler maintained a
highly productive greenhouse complex in this area.

Walden Pond State Reservation   To reach Walden Pond from the
Concord Depot, continue down Thoreau Street past the depot and
through the intersection of Thoreau and Sudbury Road. A little more
than half a mile from the depot, Thoreau Street ends at Walden Street,
where the visitor should turn right. (Turning left leads back to the
business district of Concord Center.) Just past the **Hapgood Wright
Town Forest** entrance (on the left) and **Thoreau's Path on Brister's Hill**
(a self-guided interpretive trail maintained by the Walden Woods Project), there is a traffic light where Walden Street crosses over Route 2,
beyond which it becomes Route 126. About half a mile from the intersection of Thoreau and Walden, Walden Pond State Reservation will
be on the visitor's right, the parking lot for it on the left.

   There is a replica of the Walden cabin that Thoreau occupied
between 1845 and 1847 near the parking lot for the reservation. Within the reservation proper (across Route 126 from the parking area),
the site of Thoreau's cabin is well-marked and easily accessible by
footpath. Visitors are requested to minimize erosion by staying on the
paths and not disturbing the vegetation.

   Pilgrims to Walden occasionally express surprise that the pond
displays gentle rather than majestic beauty. Indeed, Walden's fame rests
not so much in its actual landscape as in its importance to Concord's
nineteenth-century authors, and to Thoreau in particular.

Sun Sparkles on Walden, *October 21, 1920, by Herbert Wendell Gleason*

Born in Concord in 1817, Henry David Thoreau was a Transcendentalist, author, lecturer, naturalist, student of Native American artifacts and life, surveyor, pencil maker, active opponent of slavery, social critic, and reformer. Having for some time mulled over the idea of living in nature, in March 1845 he began cutting pines for lumber to build a cabin on Ralph Waldo Emerson's land at Walden Pond. He moved in on July 4, 1845. Between that time and his departure from Walden on September 6, 1847, Thoreau lived self-sufficiently, as he wrote in the first paragraph of his book *Walden; or, Life in the Woods* (first published in 1854), "earning my living by the labor of my hands only." He fished and grew beans. He focused on essentials and spent whatever time was not required to obtain them observing and writing about the world around and within. He visited family and friends in town often, and they visited him. While living at the pond, he was arrested and briefly jailed for nonpayment of the poll tax in protest against government complicity in slavery through war with Mexico. Thoreau left Walden in 1847 with the completed manuscript of the book *A Week on the Concord and Merrimack Rivers* (published 1849) and with much material that would eventually form his *Walden,* as well.

Because of Thoreau's two-year residence at Walden, the pond quickly became—in the words of nineteenth-century Concord guidebook writer George Bradford Bartlett—"one of the most noted sheets of water in America." (Bartlett's *Concord Guide Book*—the first full-length guidebook devoted to the town—appeared in 1880, and was revised and reissued many times.) Over time, *Walden* familiarized countless readers with the pond and imbued it with spiritual as well as concrete properties. In 1872, Bronson Alcott and Mrs. Mary Newbury Adams of Dubuque, Iowa, placed the first stones of a cairn to memorialize Thoreau and his experiment in deliberate living. In 1922, descendants of Ralph Waldo Emerson and others deeded the Commonwealth of Massachusetts their property at Walden to preserve "the Walden of Emerson and Thoreau, its shores and nearby woodlands for the public who wish to enjoy the Pond, the woods [and] nature, including bathing, boating, fishing, and picnicking." The Middlesex County Commissioners managed the reservation until the state took control in 1975. In 1945, archaeologist Roland Wells Robbins identified the location of Thoreau's Walden cabin more accurately than suggested by the cairn.

Walden has not always presented an idyllic face. Protecting it from damaging overuse has proven difficult. In his guide to Concord, Bartlett wrote of Walden as "a pellucid basin of the purest water nestling among low hills," and declared that its "rare and lovely beauty attracted alike the poet, philosopher, and naturalist." A few pages later, however, he described in detail the picnic, swimming, and athletic areas created after the Fitchburg Railroad purchased land on the side of the pond nearest the railroad track, in 1866. The railroad brought in sand to improve the beach. Bathhouses were built, a path made around the pond, and swings, see-saws, merry-go-rounds, and pavilions for speakers constructed. Paths were cut through the woods, and fields for football and baseball as well as a racetrack added. Boats took visitors out onto the pond, and a wooden footbridge facilitated crossing the tracks.

Lake Walden (as the pond was commonly called in its amusement park period) was a convenient day-trip by train from Boston and a popular destination for thousands. Needless to say, those who remembered the solitude of Thoreau's Walden were disturbed by the crowds drawn to the place. Although the amusement park burned at the beginning of the twentieth century, its presence had from the outset alarmed those who felt that Walden should be appreciated on Thoreau's idealistic terms. The later work of conservation organizations like the Thoreau Society's Save Walden Committee (which successfully protested invasive landscape alterations by the Middlesex County Commissioners in the late 1950s), Walden Forever Wild, the Thoreau Country Conservation Alliance, and the Walden Woods Project demonstrates the persistent tension between stewardship and use.

Walden Pond was designated a National Historic Landmark in 1965. The Walden Pond State Reservation—encompassing Walden Pond itself (a glacial kettle hole pond) and considerable undeveloped acreage surrounding it—is managed today by the Massachusetts Department of Conservation and Recreation (DCR) as part of the state's state's Office of Energy and Environmental Affairs. The reservation attracts those who admire the life, thought, and work of Henry David Thoreau, those who seek spirit in nature, naturalists, environmentalists, and those invigorated by outdoor activities—walking, jogging, swimming, boating, fishing, picnicking, cross-country skiing, and snowshoeing. Hundreds of thousands of people now visit Walden annually.

While access to the pond and its surroundings is free, visitors should be forewarned that parking requires payment of a fee. Only 1000 people may be in the reservation at a time. A boat ramp is available for public use. Bicycles are not permitted within the reservation, nor are dogs, barbecue grills, alcoholic beverages, novelty inflation devices, metal detectors, camping, gasoline engines, wind-powered sailcraft, hunting, or parking on the road. Lifeguards are posted throughout the summer to ensure swimmer safety. The reservation is open year-round, from 5:00 A.M. to half an hour after sunset, with some variation in hours. For additional information and regulations and to find out about upcoming programs, consult the Walden Pond State Reservation Web pages at http://www.mass.gov/eea/agencies/dcr/massparks/region-north/walden-pond-state-reservation.html. A map is available on the website, and (in printed form) at the DCR Visitors Center (a building located on the same side of Route 126 where parking for Walden Pond is located, just a little beyond the entrance to the parking lot as approached from Concord Center; the official address is 915 Walden Street). To arrange for an organized group visit, call the office at (978) 369-3254.

Through its Friends of Walden Pond, the Thoreau Society helps to support park programming and operations. The Thoreau Society Shop at Walden Pond shares the DCR office building at 915 Walden Street. The shop offers Thoreau-related books, artwork, clothing, souvenirs, and other items for sale.

Having taken in Walden Pond, the visitor may return to Monument Square by heading back on Route 126 toward Route 2, crossing Route 2, and continuing down Walden Street to Main Street in the center of town. A right turn on Main will lead directly to the Square.

Lexington Road

Leaving Monument Square, Lexington Road is flanked by the Wright Tavern on the right and the Hill Burying Ground on the left. The original Concord house lots granted by the General Court of the Massachusetts Bay Colony were located along the stretch of this road beginning just beyond the cemetery. The dugout homes that sheltered the first settlers here were built into the ridge that runs above it, to the left. The present Lexington Road was a part of the Bay Road from Boston in the seventeenth and eighteenth centuries. In April 1775, British troops followed it as they marched to and from town. It was later known as the Boston Road or the County Road. During the nineteenth century, authors Ralph Waldo Emerson, Bronson and Louisa May Alcott, and Nathaniel Hawthorne made their homes on it. Today, some of Concord's oldest houses and several key historic sites open to visitors are contained within the span of Lexington Road known as the "American Mile."

Meeting house of the First Parish in Concord, prior to 1900 fire and rebuilding

First Parish   Located to the right just after the Wright Tavern, the
First Parish at 20 Lexington Road is the Unitarian Universalist
descendant of Concord's original church, which was gathered in 1636
in Cambridge. First ministers Peter Bulkeley and John Jones were
installed in 1637. The original meeting house was built on the hill on
the opposite side of Lexington Road from the present location of the
church. A second meeting house was built between 1667 and 1673
across the road from its predecessor, a third in 1711. The third meeting house, renovated in 1791 and again in 1841 (when it was turned
ninety degrees to face Lexington Road instead of the town center),
burned to the ground in April 1900. A fourth meeting house, which
still stands today, was built to replace and—as much as possible—to
reproduce the old building.

Ministers of the First Parish include three ancestors of Ralph
Waldo Emerson—Concord founder Peter Bulkeley and eighteenth-
century clergymen Daniel Bliss and William Emerson—and also his
step-grandfather, Ezra Ripley. From 1970 until 1986, the distinguished
Dana McLean Greeley—former minister at the Arlington Street Church
in Boston, last president of the American Unitarian Association, and
founding president of the Unitarian Universalist Association—was
minister here.

During the ministry of the evangelical Daniel Bliss, a group of
parishioners left to form their own church, which met at the Black
Horse Tavern, on what is now the site of the Concord Free Public
Library. In 1774 and 1775, the meeting house of the First Parish
was used for sessions of the Provincial Congress, in 1775 and 1776
for Harvard College classes (temporarily moved from Cambridge to
Concord in wartime). During Ezra Ripley's long ministry (from 1778
to 1841), the First Parish became Unitarian. In 1826, a group desir-
ing a more conservative form of worship broke away from the First
Parish to establish Concord's Trinitarian Congregational Church. The
First Parish has been Unitarian Universalist since 1961, when the American Unitarian Association merged with the Universalist Church of
America, forming the Unitarian Universalist Association.

Over the years, the church building has accommodated a variety
of non-parish purposes. During the nineteenth century, some of the
meetings of the Concord Lyceum were held in it. Lectures and other

programs still take place here. Each July, the Thoreau Society meets at the church for the business session of its Annual Gathering.

From Concord's settlement well into the nineteenth century, church and state were one, and parish business was conducted at town meeting. Although the official separation of church and state took place in Massachusetts in 1834, the First Parish did not separate from the municipal government of Concord until the mid-1850s. The first annual parish meeting independent of town government was held in 1856.

In addition to the meeting house and the land it occupies on Lexington Road, the First Parish also owns the Wright Tavern and houses on the Church Green (the lane off Lexington Road just beyond the church).

Pellet-Barrett House (former D.A.R. Chapter House) A number of antique houses on both sides of Lexington Road are still private residences. Among them is the Pellet-Barrett House at 5–7, 13/15 Lexington Road (on the left when exiting Monument Square). Located roughly across the road from the First Parish, this house may incorporate one of the oldest structures in Concord. Daniel Pellet (or Pellett) owned the property on which it stands and a small house here from the late 1690s into the early eighteenth century. His seventeenth-century house is believed to survive as an ell on the present building, which was enlarged in the eighteenth century. In the twentieth century, the Pellet House provided a chapter house for the Old Concord Chapter of the Daughters of the American Revolution. It is today—as it was originally —a private home.

Concord Art-John Ball House Once a residence, the eighteenth-century John Ball House at 37 Lexington Road is now open to the public as a gallery. Thought to have been a stop on the Underground Railroad in the nineteenth century, the Ball House is today the home of Concord Art (formerly the Concord Art Association). Founded in 1917 by Philadelphia-born Concord artist Elizabeth Wentworth Roberts (an impressionist painter who studied in Europe), the Concord Art Association moved into the house in 1922. Sculptor Daniel Chester French—creator of the *Minute Man* statue unveiled in 1875 at the reconstructed North Bridge—served as president of the association. Devoted to encouraging and promoting the visual arts, Concord Art offers frequently changing exhibitions of work by area artists, lectures, classes, and trips to museums and exhibitions, and also maintains a small permanent collection.

Concord Art is open regular hours Tuesday through Saturday for visitors to its galleries. (Sunday hours are more limited than those for the rest of the week.) Admission is free. For additional information, call (978) 369-2578, or visit the association's website at www.concordart.org.

Reuben Brown House Heading toward the Emerson House, the Concord Museum, Orchard House, and The Wayside (all sites open to the public), the visitor will pass the privately-owned, early eighteenth-century Reuben Brown House at 77 Lexington Road, on the left side of the road. During the Revolution, the house was occupied by Reuben Brown, a saddler, harness maker, and lieutenant in one of the local military companies. On April 19, 1775, Brown was ordered to ride toward Boston to determine the accuracy of the report that British troops were on their way to Concord. He reached Lexington just as the British fired on the militia there. He returned to Concord and was subsequently sent out as an alarm rider to spread word of the gunfire at Lexington and of the British advance on Concord. Brown's shop was set on fire that day but the blaze was put out before extensive damage was done.

From 1887 until 1930, the collection of the Concord Antiquarian Society (predecessor of the Concord Museum) was stored and displayed in the Reuben Brown House, which is now—again—a private home.

Heywood Meadow and Gun House Heywood Street meets Lexington Road a short distance beyond the Reuben Brown House, across Lexington Road, to the visitor's right. Heywood Meadow, an expanse of largely undeveloped land, is located on both sides of Heywood Street, most of it on the side farthest from the town center. The Mill Brook runs through the meadow. In the seventeenth century, Concord settler Luke Potter had a house at what is now the Heywood Street/Lexington Road intersection—probably the first house built on the Mill Brook side rather than the ridge side of the Bay Road. Although buildings on it have come and gone, Heywood Meadow has been maintained mainly as open or agricultural space since the seventeenth century. Its inviting greenway quality survived private ownership by the Potter, Beatton, Prescott, Fay, and Heywood families prior to town acquisition; an unsuccessful attempt in 1969 by the Middlesex County Commissioners to take it by eminent domain for the construction of a district courthouse; and the location on it of the old Concord Information Booth (forerunner of the present Visitor Center at 58 Main Street) from 1966 through 2001. Heywood Meadow still offers a quiet place for the visitor to spread a blanket, have lunch, and reflect.

The brick gun house of the Concord Independent Battery is located at the far end of Heywood Meadow, near the Cambridge Turnpike. Dedicated on April 19, 1961, the gun house (not open to the public) holds the two brass cannon regularly fired as part of Concord's Patriots' Day and Memorial Day celebrations. The Concord Independent Battery descends from the Concord Artillery. The Artillery was established in 1804 to honor the heroism on April 19, 1775, of Major John Buttrick of Concord and Captain Isaac Davis of Acton. It served ceremonial and social functions—parade duty on April 19 chief among them—as well as military. When Massachusetts reorganized its militia system in 1840, the Concord Artillery continued under a new command. The Town of Concord subsequently assumed greater responsibility for maintaining the Artillery, which played an increasingly important role in public ceremonies and celebrations. The Artillery eventually became known as the Concord Independent Battery. In 1947, the Concord Independent Battery Association was established to support and promote the Battery as a local, proudly patriotic institution.

The Town of Concord's Emerson-Thoreau Amble begins in the Heywood Meadow/gun house vicinity.

Emerson House Continuing east on Lexington Road past Heywood Meadow, the visitor will quickly come to the Cambridge Turnpike, on the right. The Emerson House is located at the intersection of the two roads, at 28 Cambridge Turnpike, on the right side of the road.

Nineteenth-century philosopher, essayist, lecturer, poet, and sometime minister Ralph Waldo Emerson was during his lifetime and remains today Concord's most locally respected resident. He was born and raised in Boston, but his roots here were deep. His ancestry extended back to

*Emerson House on the Cambridge Turnpike, between 1890 and 1895,
by Alfred Winslow Hosmer*

Concord's Colonial origins and was intertwined with the history of the First Parish. During their childhood, Emerson and his brothers stayed in Concord at the Old Manse, home of their step-grandfather, the Reverend Ezra Ripley. Ralph Waldo developed a lasting fondness for Concord that in 1834 led him back to settle permanently.

Born in 1803, Emerson was just eight years old when his father William, a minister in Boston, died, leaving his wife and children financially constrained. Nevertheless, Ruth Haskins Emerson managed to educate her sons. Ralph Waldo Emerson graduated from Harvard College in 1821. He entered Harvard Divinity School in 1825, married his first wife, Ellen Tucker, in 1829, and lost her to tuberculosis in 1831. He resigned from his pastorate at the Second Church in Boston in September 1832, and in December of that year traveled to Europe, where he met Wordsworth, Coleridge, and Carlyle. He returned to America in 1833 to take up a new career as a lecturer. In 1834, his brother Edward died. Shortly thereafter, Emerson moved into the Manse. There he worked on a book that he had been thinking about for some time. When finally published in 1836, *Nature* launched his literary career and unleashed a period of intense expression of Transcendental thought and reaction to it.

Emerson became engaged to Lydia Jackson of Plymouth early in 1835. When the couple considered the matter of where they would live, Emerson made his best case for Concord. Resolute in his preference for Concord over Plymouth, he prevailed. In the summer of 1835, he bought the house on the Cambridge Turnpike where he and Lydia—whom he renamed Lidian after their marriage—would begin family life. They were married in Plymouth in September, shortly after Emerson delivered his address at the bicentennial celebration of Concord's incorporation. The next day, Emerson brought his bride to the home they first called Coolidge House or Coolidge Castle after its original owner (Charles Coolidge), and later renamed Bush. The Emersons made alterations to it in 1836 and 1857. The 1836 renovation provided two rooms meant for Emerson's brother Charles and Elizabeth Hoar, who were to be married in September 1836. The rooms were never used for their intended purpose, however. Charles died in May of that year.

In this house, the Emerson children were born—Waldo in 1836, Ellen Tucker (named for Emerson's first wife) in 1839, Edith in 1841, Edward Waldo in 1844. Young Waldo died here of scarlet fever in January 1842. In 1865, daughter Edith married William H. Forbes, Jr., in the parlor. Henry Thoreau lived here with the Emerson family as handyman and caretaker at two different periods in the 1840s. Relatives and friends visited and sometimes stayed at the house for long periods of time. Authors, publishers, radical thinkers, and social reformers came to converse with Concord's resident philosopher. And here Emerson died in 1882.

Emerson's original purchase included house, barn, and about two acres of land. Other parcels were later added. Something of a gentleman farmer, Emerson planted fruit trees on his property and regularly displayed pears at the Middlesex Agricultural Society's annual exhibition. He also set out pine and hemlock trees.

The Emerson house as it now appears is as reconstructed following a devastating fire in July 1872. Due to quick action by neighbors and townsfolk, much was saved, including many of Emerson's manuscripts and books. With the assistance of his good friend Judge Ebenezer Rockwood Hoar, space for a study for Emerson was obtained in the courthouse on Monument Square. Moreover, Emerson's friends collected and presented him with funds sufficient to restore the house and to travel abroad while repairs were in progress.

After moving into the house on the Cambridge Turnpike in 1835, Emerson assumed the role of Concord's most prominent citizen. His Concord heritage and his characteristic humility and inclination to deal kindly with others—no matter what their social status—made local residents feel that he was one of them. In 1837, his "Concord Hymn," written at the request of the town, was sung at the dedication of the Battle Monument near the site where the North Bridge had stood. Over the years, he served the town through its lyceum, as a member of its School Committee and Library Committee, through attendance at town meetings, and as a public speaker on many occasions.

Those who formed part of Emerson's Transcendental circle were frequent guests in his home. Moreover, unknown visitors from all over often came to Concord just for the opportunity of meeting one of the most recognized men in America. But Concordians knew and appreciated Emerson within the context of town life. Despite the demands made upon him as a lecturer and a man of letters, Emerson was invested in Concord's day-to-day life and the management of local affairs. The people of the town responded by accepting him as one of their own—even when his ideas and actions generated controversy, and even though some admitted that they did not comprehend the philosophical issues he pondered. He was an influential man, but he radiated an encompassing sense of democracy that appealed to his Yankee townsmen. Emerson derived comfort and satisfaction from his place in Concord as a community. The warm and mutual feeling between Emerson and Concord affected the town as well. Concord is what it is now in large part because it was the chosen home of one of the most influential thinkers of the nineteenth century.

After the death in 1930 of Edward Waldo Emerson (the Emersons' youngest child), the Ralph Waldo Emerson Memorial Association was formed to maintain and manage the Emerson house and property. The house remains today much as it was at the end of Ralph Waldo Emerson's life, with the exception of the contents of his study, which were transferred to the Concord Antiquarian Society (now the Concord Museum) in the early 1930s.

The Emerson House is open Thursday through Sunday April through October (Sundays in the afternoon only). For additional information, call the Emerson House at (978) 369-2236.

Concord Museum The Concord Museum is located at the intersection of Lexington Road and the Cambridge Turnpike. The entrance to and parking lot for it are on the Cambridge Turnpike, diagonally opposite the Emerson House. Through self-touring galleries, period rooms, the exhibition "Why Concord?," and an accompanying orientation film, the museum provides a comprehensive interpretation of Concord history from Native American inhabitation to the present time. It also offers special exhibitions on subjects that intersect with aspects of Concord history. The Concord Museum represents local material culture through a distinguished collection of Concord-made or Concord-owned objects, which showcase the decorative arts of the seventeenth, eighteenth, and nineteenth centuries, including furniture, clocks, textiles, ceramics, tableware, and metalware. The museum's Revolutionary-era holdings include powder horns, muskets, and fifes associated with the Concord Fight; one of the two lanterns hung in the belfry of the Old North Church on April 18, 1775, to signal the route (land or sea) that the British would take at the beginning of their expedition to Lexington and Concord; and a diorama of the Concord Fight. Nineteenth-century holdings include Ralph Waldo Emerson's study, transferred from the Emerson House in the 1930s, and over two hundred artifacts associated with Henry Thoreau, among them the furniture he used in his cabin at Walden Pond between 1845 and 1847.

The Concord Museum evolved from the Concord Antiquarian Society, which was established in 1886 by a group of Concordians devoted to preserving and promoting local history. The collection of antiquarian Cummings E. Davis formed the nucleus around which the society's holdings grew over time. In 1887, the organization purchased the Reuben Brown House on Lexington Road, where it stored and displayed its collection until moving in 1930 to its present location, into a building designed by noted Concord architect Harry Britton Little and later expanded. In the first decade of the twentieth century, the society organized its holdings into period room groupings. In 1911, it published a catalog of its collection, prepared by its secretary, George

Tolman, a local antiquarian and genealogist. Beginning in 1930, the collection expanded significantly through gifts by Russell Hawes Kettell, an expert on and collector of early American furniture. In the latter part of the twentieth century, the Concord Antiquarian Society became known as the Concord Museum. In 1991, it opened a new two-story wing designed by Cambridge architect Graham Gund.

The Concord Museum is handicapped accessible, open three hundred sixty-two days a year, offers a variety of public and school programs, and maintains a shop. For hours, admission fees, programs, events, and membership information, consult the museum's website at www.concordmuseum.org. For additional information or to schedule a group visit, call (978) 369-9763 or send an e-mail to cm1@concordmuseum.org or grouptours@concordmuseum.org. Taped information is accessible by calling (978) 369-9609.

Moore Farmhouse Back on Lexington Road, the visitor will see the Moore Farmhouse, a private home at 343-355 Lexington, on the left, just beyond the Cambridge Turnpike. Its particular significance in relation to the events of April 19, 1775, lies in the fact that it either incorporates or was built upon the site of the eighteenth-century residence of Dr. Samuel Prescott, who carried to Concord word that the king's troops were on the road here after Paul Revere and William Dawes were thwarted in the attempt by a British patrol. (Revere was captured, Dawes turned back.) In the first half of the nineteenth century, the structure now on the site was home to Abel Moore when he retired from service in Concord as Middlesex County deputy sheriff and jailer. Moore farmed here, and his farm was eventually taken over by his son, John Brooks Moore, a progressive horticulturist who successfully developed and marketed grape varieties and grew a number of fruits and vegetables—strawberries and asparagus among them—in quantity.

Orchard House and Concord School of Philosophy Louisa May Alcott's Orchard House and the Concord School of Philosophy are located at 399 Lexington Road, just beyond the Moore Farmhouse, on the same side of the street. Visitors may use the small parking area directly in front of Orchard House, or the parking lot maintained by Minute Man National Historical Park across Lexington Road, on Hawthorne Lane.

In September 1857, educator, philosopher, lecturer, poet, essayist, diarist, and reformer Amos Bronson Alcott wrote from Boston to his daughters about his possible purchase of a Concord home "adjoining Hillside [an earlier home of the Alcotts], under the Elms and butternuts, embowered in a thrifty apple orchard . . . The house is old, but still habitable, and with some repairs might do till our means enabled us to make it what we want."

The house had been built early in the eighteenth century. The ownership history of the property on which it stood went back to the seventeenth century, to Concord settler Edward Wright. In 1672, the parcel was acquired by John Hoar, who took responsibility for housing the Christian Indians in Concord during King Philip's War. (Hoar is remembered for ransoming Mary Rowlandson, wife of the minister of Lancaster, Massachusetts, who was held captive by the Native Americans after the attack on Lancaster in February 1676.) The house that evolved on the site remained in the Hoar family into the nineteenth century, when it was purchased by John Brooks Moore, who sold it to Bronson Alcott in 1857.

The old structure was run-down when the Alcotts acquired it. Extensive work was required to rehabilitate and expand Orchard House (the family's name for the place, which Louisa Alcott—then in her mid-twenties—more subversively dubbed "Apple Slump"). While it was being readied, the family lived first in lodgings on Bedford Street (in a building that no longer stands) and then, with renovations in the spring of 1858 making closer supervision advisable, in part of the Hawthorne's Wayside (the former Hillside), next door to Orchard House. (The Hawthornes were abroad following Nathaniel Hawthorne's consulship in Liverpool.)

Between the time the Alcotts bought Orchard House and their taking up residence in July 1858, major changes occurred within the family, which included four daughters, Anna, Louisa, Elizabeth (Lizzie), and May. Lizzie died in March 1858. A few weeks later, Anna announced her engagement to John Bridge Pratt, one of the friends with whom the Alcott girls socialized and produced amateur theatricals.

During their residence in the house, Bronson, Louisa, and May (an artist) pursued their respective callings with determination. Bronson's particular interests and talents were locally recognized between 1859 and 1865, when he served Concord as Superintendent of Schools.

Moreover, he eventually found a receptive audience on the lecture circuit, and took enormous satisfaction in his Concord School of Philosophy. Sessions of the school brought lecturers and audiences to Concord every summer between 1879 and 1887 to explore philosophy, celebrate literature, and keep the flame of Transcendental idealism burning, and embodied Mr. Alcott's commitment to dialogue as a means of life-long learning. (The sole program for the 1888 season was a memorial service in June for Bronson Alcott, who died in March of that year.) In 1880, the Hillside Chapel was built for these summer sessions. Today, the building is still used for programs and lectures.

Encouraged by Thomas Niles of the Boston publishing firm of Roberts Brothers, Louisa achieved enormous reputation and financial security with the publication in two parts (1868 and 1869) of her blockbuster book for girls, *Little Women*, which drew on Alcott family

Orchard House, ca. 1870, from stereographic print

life. On and off, when home responsibilities prevented her from concentrating on her writing, Louisa left Concord to stay in Boston, where she could work without distraction.

May honed her skills as an artist while living in Orchard House, which presented her with a ready-made canvas for the exercise of her aesthetic sensibilities and emerging skills. She sketched outline figures from various sources in pencil, ink, and paint on walls and trim, most abundantly in her own bedroom, in ornamenting which she traced and copied from John Flaxman's illustrations for the *Iliad* and the *Odyssey* and from Guido Reni's *Aurora*. Visitors may still see May's work on her bedroom walls and displayed elsewhere in the house. May traveled to Europe to study art three times in the 1870s. She married in London in 1878 (on her third trip abroad), and died in Paris in 1879.

The Alcotts remained at Orchard House until 1877, when they moved to Main Street, to the "Yellow House" formerly occupied by the Thoreau family. Mrs. Alcott—a woman of patience and conscience, an active reformer and good neighbor, and in many ways the glue that held the family together—died a short time after the move.

Orchard House is a National Historic Landmark. A visit to it opens a window into the mid-nineteenth-century world the Alcotts knew, inspires appreciation of the strength of their family bonds, and encourages understanding of the intellectual and social currents that influenced them.

Owned and operated by the Louisa May Alcott Memorial Association, Orchard House is open year-round for guided tours and programs. Groups of ten or more must make reservations in advance. There is a museum shop that sells gifts, craft items, books, and cards. For details about hours, fees, and upcoming workshops and programs (including the Summer Conversational Series), visit the Orchard House website at http://www.louisamayalcott.org/. To contact a staff member, e-mail info@louisamayalcott.org or phone (978) 369-4118.

The Wayside   Directly east of Orchard House, The Wayside at 455 Lexington Road forms part of Minute Man National Historical Park. It is significant as the residence of Revolutionary muster master Samuel Whitney and, later, of authors Amos Bronson Alcott, Louisa May Alcott, Nathaniel Hawthorne, and Margaret Sidney.

From 1769 to 1778, storekeeper Samuel Whitney owned this house, an early Colonial structure altered and expanded over time. At Concord's January 27, 1775, town meeting, Whitney was chosen to serve as muster master of the "Minute Company Lat[e]ly . . . inlisted in this Town." He was also a delegate to the Provincial Congress, and ammunition was stored on his property. On April 19, 1775, British troops passed his house as they marched into Concord in search of hidden arms and provisions, and again on their retreat after the confrontation at the North Bridge.

Following Whitney's ownership, the house was sold five times before its purchase in 1845 by Transcendental thinker, educational and social reformer, and author Amos Bronson Alcott and his wife, Abigail May Alcott. In 1843, the Alcotts had moved to Harvard, Massachusetts, where Bronson Alcott and English reformer Charles Lane established Fruitlands, a utopian community. Impractical farmers, Alcott

The Wayside, ca. 1870, from card stereograph

and Lane found it difficult to sustain the operation and to maintain a tolerable standard of living for Mrs. Alcott and her daughters. The Alcotts left Fruitlands in January 1844. Louisa, second of the four Alcott girls, was twelve when her family bought the old Whitney house in 1845 with help from her father's friend, Ralph Waldo Emerson. They named their new home "Hillside." Bronson extensively repaired, renovated, and enlarged the house, and worked on the garden, well, yard, hillside terraces, and outbuildings. The family remained here until 1848.

Because the Alcotts were strongly opposed to slavery, their Hillside was a stop on the Underground Railroad. Hillside was also the real-life setting for many of the events that Louisa May Alcott later fictionalized in *Little Women*, even though the book was written while the family lived next door, at Orchard House.

The Alcotts leased Hillside from 1848 until 1852, when they sold it to author Nathaniel Hawthorne. Born in Salem, Hawthorne lived in Concord during three periods of his life—from 1842 to 1845 at the Old Manse (which inspired his *Mosses from an Old Manse*, published in 1846), and from 1852 to 1853 and 1860 to 1864 in the Lexington Road house purchased from the Alcotts. Between their departure from the Manse in 1845 and their return to Concord in 1852, the Hawthornes lived first in Salem, where Hawthorne served as Surveyor in the Custom House; then in Lenox (in the Berkshires), where he became a friend of Herman Melville; then in West Newton.

By the time Hawthorne took office in Salem, he had engaged as broad an audience as possible for an author lacking the security and marketing expertise of a regular publisher. His situation changed radically after his dismissal from the Salem Custom House in 1849. Gathering together a new collection of tales for publication, he planned to include a long story titled "The Scarlet Letter." James T. Fields of the Boston literary publishing house of Ticknor, Reed, and Fields visited Hawthorne in 1849. Hawthorne gave the manuscript collection to Fields, who singled out "The Scarlet Letter" as worthy of development into a full-length romance. With the publication and immediate success of *The Scarlet Letter* in 1850, Ticknor, Reed, and Fields (later Ticknor and Fields) became Hawthorne's primary publisher for the rest of his life. In rapid succession between 1850 and 1853, the company issued not only Hawthorne's *The Scarlet Letter* but also his *True Stories from History and Biography, The House of the Seven Gables, A Wonder-Book for Girls and Boys, The Snow-Image, The Blithedale Romance,* and *Tanglewood Tales.*

In June 1852, Nathaniel and Sophia Hawthorne moved back to Concord with their three children (Una, Julian, and Rose), to the refurbished Alcott house on Lexington Road, which Hawthorne renamed The Wayside. Hawthorne particularly valued the seclusion of the hill behind his new house, where he walked, deep in thought, along the ridge. Soon after the move to The Wayside, Hawthorne's college friend Franklin Pierce, the Democratic nominee for the presidency, asked him to write a campaign biography. Hawthorne complied, Pierce won the election in November, and Hawthorne was subsequently appointed the American consul in Liverpool. The Hawthornes sailed from Boston in July 1853.

Hawthorne held the consulship until late 1857. From 1858 into 1860, he and his family traveled on the Continent, lingering in Italy. They returned to England, then in June 1860 came back to Concord. While the family was abroad, The Wayside was occupied by Sophia Hawthorne's brother Nathaniel Peabody and (later) the widowed Mary Peabody Mann (Sophia's sister; Mrs. Horace Mann) and her children.

Hawthorne had completed only one book—*The Marble Faun*—during his seven years abroad. Back in Concord, he undertook landscape improvements and the expansion of the cramped Wayside, including the addition of his tower study, with a standing desk. He resumed writing soon after resettling here. He wrote a series of sketches of English people, places, and life, published between 1860 and 1863 in the *Atlantic Monthly* and collected in 1863 under the title *Our Old Home.* Depressed by the Civil War and in deteriorating health, he was unable to complete another romance. He died in 1864. Hawthorne's family remained at The Wayside until the fall of 1868, and sold the place in 1870.

During the 1870s, The Wayside was used as a school for girls. In 1879, Hawthorne's youngest daughter Rose and her husband George Parsons Lathrop bought it. Devastated by the death in 1881 of their only child, in 1883 the Lathrops sold it to publisher Daniel Lothrop

and his wife Harriett Mulford Lothrop, author of the "Five Little Pepper" books, which she wrote under the pen name Margaret Sidney.
Their daughter Margaret was born at The Wayside in 1884. Keenly
aware of the historical importance of the house, the Lothrops made
few changes. Having purchased it as a summer place, they occupied
it intermittently. Daniel Lothrop died in 1892, Harriett in 1924.
Margaret Lothrop subsequently leased the house. In 1932, she returned to live in it, opening it to the public during summers. She was
determined to find some way of preserving it as a historic site accessible to the public. In 1963, The Wayside was designated a National
Historic Landmark. In 1965, the National Park Service purchased it
from Miss Lothrop and added it to the recently-established Minute
Man National Historical Park.

The Park Service maintains a visitor parking lot on Hawthorne
Lane, which forms a tee intersection with Lexington Road diagonally
across from both Orchard House and The Wayside. There is an interpretive exhibit in the barn adjacent to The Wayside. Current hours,
fees, and other information may be obtained by phoning park headquarters at (978) 369-6993 or checking the Minute Man National
Historical Park website at http://www.nps.gov/mima/index.htm.

Grapevine Cottage Ephraim Bull's "Grapevine Cottage" is located
at 491 Lexington Road, just beyond Orchard House and The Wayside, on the same side of the road. An early eighteenth-century building with later additions, it remains a private home. A goldbeater by

Ephraim Wales Bull, 1880s

trade, Bull is best remembered for his
avocation, the cultivation of grapes.
While living here, he bred roses and
experimented with wild grapes, developing the hardy Concord Grape
in 1849. He produced other grape
varieties as well, but none so successful as the Concord, which is the most
widely cultivated grape in the United
States. However, unlike his neighbor
John Brooks Moore, Bull did not
profit from his viticultural advances.
The Concord Grape was put on the

market by C. M. Hovey and Company of Boston in 1854, and its subsequent sale quickly slipped beyond Bull's control. Many nurseries made money from it, but Bull himself died poor in 1895. The inscription on his gravestone in Sleepy Hollow Cemetery reads, "He sowed, others reaped."

Meriam's Corner Just east of Grapevine Cottage and about a mile from Concord Center, Old Bedford Road veers off from Lexington Road, to the left. On the far side of the intersection of Lexington and Old Bedford sits the Meriam House, at 34 Old Bedford Road. (The multiple variations of this old Concord name also include Merriam and Miriam.) Located on a lot held by Meriams from the seventeenth century to 1871, the house standing on the site today was likely built by Joseph Meriam about 1705. On April 19, 1775, it was occupied by Nathan Meriam—a Concord selectman—and his family.

The Meriam House is significant as a fine example of Colonial farmhouse architecture. More than that, it was at Meriam's Corner (where in April 1775 another, earlier Meriam house stood between the road and the house that Joseph Meriam had constructed) that the British retreat after the Concord Fight turned into what has frequently been called a "running battle." Gunfire broke out in the vicinity of the house, precipitating an unanticipated guerrilla-style offensive in which Colonial soldiers hid behind trees, fences, rocks, and buildings— anything that provided cover—along the road back to Boston via Lexington, firing at the British as they passed. The ensuing chaos and bloodshed on the sixteen-mile trek back constituted a greater blow to British authority and morale than did the exchanges at either Lexington or Concord.

In 1885, the Town of Concord placed one of seven markers to commemorate the two hundred and fiftieth anniversary of the town's incorporation in the stone wall along the Meriam property, on Lexington Road. The marker reads:

MERIAM'S CORNER / THE BRITISH TROOPS / RETREATING FROM THE / OLD NORTH BRIDGE / WERE HERE ATTACKED IN FLANK / BY THE MEN OF CONCORD / AND NEIGHBORING TOWNS/ AND DRIVEN UNDER A HOT FIRE / TO CHARLESTOWN.

The Meriam House was acquired by the federal government in 1987 for incorporation into Minute Man National Historical Park. At the death in 1991 of the previous owner, who held life tenancy, the Park Service assumed full control over the property. Although the house is not generally open to the public, it is used for special programs and events. In advance of the Town of Concord's Patriots' Day celebration each year, the annual Meriam's Corner Exercise is held in front of it. This solemn and simple ceremony, punctuated with fife and drum music, provides a natural opportunity for visitor access to the house. The Concord Chamber of Commerce website (http://www.concordchamberofcommerce.org) includes the Meriam's Corner Exercise in its Patriots' Day event listing.

At Meriam's Corner, the visitor with time for walking or bicycling may explore Minute Man National Historical Park's Battle Road Trail, which is accessible from the parking area at the site. This five-plus mile trail connects historic sites from Meriam's Corner to Lexington and allows visitors to experience the eighteenth-century agricultural landscape and the natural surroundings on remnants of the original Battle Road, old farm paths, new sections of pathway, and boardwalks.

Meriam's Corner, showing the Meriam House and the historical marker installed in 1885, ca. 1890, by Alfred Winslow Hosmer

Thoreau Farm (Wheeler/Minot Farmhouse)   From Meriam's Corner, the house where Henry David Thoreau was born is reached by
following Old Bedford Road for about a quarter of a mile to Virginia
Road, which comes in on the right. The Thoreau Birthplace (believed
to have been built about 1730 by John Wheeler) is located at 341
Virginia Road, about a third of a mile from the intersection of Old
Bedford and Virginia, on the left. Thoreau was born here in 1817, in
a second-floor room within the "widow's thirds" (or dower) of his
grandmother, Mary Jones Dunbar Minot (Minott), widow of Captain
Jonas Minot. In Thoreau's time, the Minot farmhouse stood where
215 Virginia Road now stands. In 1878, it was moved next door to its
present location (three hundred yards away from where it was originally constructed), and a new house was built on its old site.

Thoreau's maternal step-grandfather Jonas Minot was a prosperous farmer, a landowner in and beyond Concord, a descendant of
seventeenth-century families (Wheeler as well as Minot), a Concord
selectman, and a militia captain (until local suspicion of his loyalist
sympathies caused the loss of his captaincy). A widower, he married
the fifty-year-old widow Mary Jones Dunbar of Keene, New Hampshire, in 1798. She brought the children of her first marriage to the
Reverend Asa Dunbar to the Virginia Road household. Her daughter
Cynthia, who later married John Thoreau, spent a significant part of her
early life on the Minot farm. Later, after Jonas Minot's death in 1813,
Cynthia, John, and their growing family made use of the Widow
Minot's portion of the farmhouse, where they remained until 1818.

Thoreau wrote matter-of-factly about his birth in his journal
entry for December 27, 1855: "Born, July 12, 1817, in the *Minott
House*, on the Virginia Road, where Father occupied Grandmother's
thirds, carrying on the farm . . . Lived there about eight months." Later
(December 5, 1856), he expressed his delight in the pleasures that his
arrival in Concord afforded: "I have never got over my surprise that I
should have been born into the most estimable place in all the world,
and in the very nick of time, too."

Now listed on the National Register of Historic Places, the
Thoreau Birthplace remained a farmhouse through the late nineteenth
century and much of the twentieth. In 1997, the Town of Concord
purchased the deteriorating house and the surrounding acreage,

Thoreau Birthplace,
between 1885 and 1890,
by Alfred Winslow Hosmer

preventing destruction of the house and development of the land. In 2004, the Thoreau Farm Trust—a non-profit organization devoted to restoring and reusing the birthplace—signed a purchase and sale agreement with the Town of Concord for the house and two acres of land. The mission of the organization is to preserve Thoreau's birthplace as an educational center, community resource, and place of pilgrimage. Rehabilitation of the house was completed in 2009. More information is available on the organization's website, at http://www.thoreaufarm.org/, or by calling (978) 451-0300.

In 2009, the Thoreau Society moved its headquarters to the Thoreau Birthplace. Established in 1941, the society's mission is to promote Thoreau's life, works, and legacy, to bring admirers of Thoreau, students, and scholars together, and to maintain research collections. The society publishes two periodicals, the *Concord Saunterer* and the *Thoreau Society Bulletin*. Each July, it holds its Annual Gathering in Concord. It runs a shop year-round at Walden Pond and supports programming and operations at the Walden Pond State Reservation through its Friends of Walden Pond group. The Thoreau Society website is accessible at http://www.thoreausociety.org. The office phone number is (978) 369-5310. The society's collections are housed at the Henley Library of the Thoreau Institute at Walden Woods in Lincoln, Massachusetts (http://www.walden.org/library; (781) 259-4730).

Visitors may return to Meriam's Corner via Virginia Road and Old Bedford Road.

Minute Man Visitor Center Visitors who did not stop at the Minute Man Visitor Center of the Minute Man National Historical Park on their way into Concord may wish to cap off their visit here—to prepare to see Lexington, to purchase souvenirs or books, or simply to rest and take advantage of the facilities. To reach the Minute Man Visitor Center from Meriam's Corner, continue by car along Lexington Road to Route 2A, taking a left onto 2A. The Visitor Center is several miles up, in Lexington, just over the Lincoln/Lexington town line, on the left side of the highway. Along the way, there are parking areas at several Minute Man National Historical Park sites, including the Hartwell Tavern and the spot where Paul Revere was arrested by a British patrol early in the morning of April 19, 1775. (His two companions—William Dawes and Samuel Prescott—evaded capture.) There is also a National Park marker at Bloody Angle (or Bloody Curve) in Lincoln (on Bedford Lane at the Battle Road), where the British sustained heavy casualties in the Colonial cross fire.

There is ample parking at the Minute Man Visitor Center, but those who take advantage of it need to know that the parking lot is a considerable distance by foot from the facility itself. There is, however, separate handicapped access.

In *The American Scene* (1907), Henry James wrote of Concord as the "biggest little place in America." Visitors will discover that it is difficult to do Concord justice in a single visit. It is best to give some advance thought to which sites have personal priority before a trip, to take the time necessary to enjoy those sites while here, and to plan on coming back to see more on another visit.

LEXINGTON GUIDE

Minute Man Visitor Center Visitors with time to spend or with specialized personal interests will probably prefer to make separate trips to Lexington and Concord. The sheer number of sites in the two towns and the dispersion of these sites over the local geography make a comprehensive tour challenging. If a single whirlwind visit to both is the only option, there is some logic to beginning at the Battle Green in Lexington and proceeding to Concord, since the Lexington Fight of April 19, 1775, preceded the engagement at Concord's North Bridge. However, because Concord contains a superabundance of historic sites, allocating the latter part of a day to it barely permits the visitor to scratch the surface. But regardless of whether the sightseer takes in the Revolutionary sites of Lexington on a discrete visit or in combination with a tour of Concord, stopping at the Minute Man Visitor Center of Minute Man National Historical Park (on Route 2A, near the Lexington/Lincoln town line) and the Lexington Visitors Center on the Battle Green will facilitate the planning of a meaningful itinerary.

Fiske Hill Minute Man National Historical Park offers parking and a walking path at Fiske Hill, which is located in Lexington a short distance east on 2A from the Minute Man Visitor Center. Here, on April 19, 1775, as the demoralized regulars succumbed to the cumulative effect of injury, exhaustion, and chaos during the unremitting running battle of their withdrawal from Concord, the British column began to disintegrate. At Ebenezer Fiske's well (the site of which is accessible by foot and also by car along the Battle Road), a British regular and an Acton minute man (James Hayward) confronted and shot one another. Both men died—the British soldier at once, Hayward some hours later. The stories of such individual encounters reveal the human face and toll of the war even as it began. Provincial casualties over the course of the day (killed, wounded, and missing) have been calculated at ninety-four; British casualties numbered in the hundreds.

Lexington Visitors Center Following Route 2A from Fiske Hill to Massachusetts Avenue all the way to downtown Lexington, the visitor will come to the Lexington Visitors Center, operated by the Lexington Chamber of Commerce just across from the Battle Green, where the first blood of the American Revolution was shed. If approaching Lexington via Route 95, take Exit 31A and make a right from the exit onto Bedford Street (Routes 4 and 225). After three traffic lights, Bedford Street runs into Massachusetts Avenue. The Lexington Visitors Center is located at 1875 Massachusetts Avenue, on the left side of the street. If approaching via Route 93 or the Massachusetts Turnpike, take the exit from either of those roads for Route 95 and proceed as described above. Coming from the east (Boston and Cambridge) on Route 2, take Exit 54 for Waltham Street, turning right on Waltham and continuing into Lexington Center. If traveling Route 2 from the west (Concord), take the Spring Street exit, follow Spring Street to Marrett Road, turn left onto Marrett and proceed for a little over a mile to Lincoln Street, and take a right onto Lincoln, which leads into downtown Lexington. Lexington is also accessible by public transportation (Red Line to Alewife Station and from there MBTA Bus 62, which runs to Bedford via Lexington; also, MBTA Bus 76 runs from Alewife through Lexington to the Hanscom Air Force Base).

Visitor parking is available in spaces around the Battle Green and in the Depot Square public parking lot (a short distance east on Massachusetts Avenue from the Battle Green).

The Lexington Visitors Center provides site brochures and directions, a diorama of the Lexington Fight (researched and laid out by Major William F. Buckley of Lexington; designed and constructed by John F. Scheid of Easton, Pennsylvania), and souvenirs and books for sale. Information about places to stay and eat and about local stores, services, events, and history is available at the center and through links from the Town of Lexington Web page at http://www.lexingtonma.gov/information-visitors. The Visitors Center is open daily year-round, Monday through Sunday, with reduced hours December through March. The phone number is (781) 862-1450.

Visitors on foot need not walk far to find a meal in Lexington's vibrant downtown area.

Liberty Ride The Liberty Ride—a trolley tour of Lexington and Concord—leaves at regularly scheduled times and makes multiple stops in both towns. Developed by the Lexington Tourism Committee, the ride originates at the Lexington Visitors Center at 1875 Massachusetts Avenue. It operates from the weekend before Patriots' Day through October (daily from the Saturday of Memorial Day weekend through the end of October). Additional information about Liberty Ride schedule, fees, and itinerary is available on the Web at http://www.libertyride.us/libertyride.html or by calling (781) 698-4586 for a recording. There is also a link on the Liberty Ride homepage for Lexington and regional event schedules (http://tourlexington.us/calendar.html).

Lexington maintains a handicapped-accessible minibus system, comprising six routes that depart from and return to Depot Square (see http://www.lexingtonma.gov/lexpress), and a good system of bicycle routes (see links from http://www.lexingtonma.gov/bicycle-advisory-committee).

Battle Green Settled in the mid-seventeenth century, Lexington was originally a part of Cambridge, and was initially known as Cambridge Farms. It became a separate parish in 1691. Its first church was built in 1692. In 1711, the private property around the church was purchased by subscription to serve as a public common, and in 1713—the year Lexington was incorporated as a town—a new meeting house was built on that land. Through the events of April 19, 1775, the triangle of land that constituted the Lexington Common (or Green) later became known as the Battle Green. On this grassy expanse, British soldiers and colonists issued the first gunfire of what would be the long struggle for American independence. Because the Green reflects the New England pattern of placing commons centrally within towns, most of Lexington's major historic sites are located close to it.

In the eighteenth century, Concord was a shire town, where sessions of the Middlesex County courts were held and other administrative functions were managed. On the eve of the Revolution, Concord had a population of approximately fifteen hundred people, roughly twice that of Lexington at the time. (Today, Lexington has a population of about thirty thousand to Concord's fifteen thousand.) In 1775, the British authorities in Boston were aware that Concord was a stronghold of Colonial rebellion. The Provincial Congress met there in 1774

and 1775, and stores of arms, ammunition, and supplies were hidden
in the town in 1775. Situated on the
road from Cambridge to Concord,
the primarily agricultural community of Lexington lay directly along
the route British soldiers followed
to Concord—their destination—on
April 18 and 19, 1775. Pivotally
placed by this circumstance of geography, impelled by their own strong
belief in their rights, and uncertain
of the intentions of the king's troops
marching toward them, Lexingto-
nians faced the British early on the
morning of April 19.

*Lexington's Battle Green readied
for celebration, April 19, 1875,
from card stereograph*

On the night of April 18, Revo-
lutionary leaders and Provincial Congress members John Hancock and
Samuel Adams were staying at the home of the Reverend Jonas Clarke
in Lexington. Paul Revere rode into Lexington around midnight to
warn Hancock and Adams—who were sure to be arrested if found by
the British—that the regulars were on their way. Fellow alarm rider
William Dawes rode separately and arrived in Lexington after Revere.
In response to Revere's warning, Captain John Parker—commander of
the Lexington militia—mustered his men on the Common and waited
for the regulars to arrive. When the troops did not make their appearance as anticipated, Parker dismissed his company. Those who lived
close by went home to await further orders, while others headed to the
Buckman Tavern, adjacent to the Common.

Realizing that the sizeable approaching British force of seven to
eight hundred men had been sent not specifically to capture Hancock
and Adams but rather primarily to seize hidden stores in Concord,
Paul Revere and William Dawes rode off to warn that town, accompanied by Dr. Samuel Prescott, who was returning home there after
visiting his lady friend in Lexington. Revere was captured en route by
a British patrol, Dawes escaped, and Prescott guided his horse over a
stone wall to carry the alarm to Concord. Revere soon talked his captors into releasing him. He headed back into Lexington to find that

Captain Parker Monument, *from* **Concord and Lexington: The Best Collection of Views** . . . *(Boston: The Worcester Press, 1908), by E. F. Worcester*

Hancock and Adams had not yet left, and saw them on their way. The British finally reached Lexington around dawn. Summoned again by alarm guns, the town bell, and the beat of the call to arms on young William Diamond's drum, the militia reassembled on the Green.

Captain Parker understood that in an armed confrontation his band of fewer than eighty men could not hope to successfully defend Lexington against the much larger British force, which was led by Lieutenant Colonel Francis Smith and Major John Pitcairn. Parker consequently ordered the militia to disperse. They began to break ranks, and gunfire erupted. Eight Americans were killed on the Green, ten wounded. One British soldier was also wounded. British arrogance at the turn of events and provincial shock over the fact that local men were shot as they scattered galvanized the colonists' sense of righteous indignation and their later determination to take the military offensive when the British no longer held the strategic advantage.

Although the question of which side fired first will probably never be answered once and for all, the meaning of the exchange at Lexington was clear from the moment it took place. Captain Parker is reported to have said to his men as they waited on the Common for the approaching British, "Stand your ground. Don't fire unless fired upon. But if they mean to have a war, let it begin here!" The action at Lexington, combined with events later that morning in Concord and the subsequent British retreat back to Boston, definitively launched the American Revolution.

The Lexington Battle Green was made a National Historic Landmark in 1962. To reach it from the Visitor Center, walk a short distance west, past the Buckman Tavern, and cross Bedford Street to the eastern point of the Green, where a memorial minute man statue in bronze stands prominently.

Lexington Minute Man Statue (Captain Parker Statue) At his death in England in 1895, Lexingtonian Francis Brown Hayes bequeathed the town ten thousand dollars to install a memorial fountain on the Battle Green. Lexington received the funds in 1898 and subsequently erected the Hayes Memorial Fountain—a bronze statue often described as depicting Captain John Parker, set on a large stone, at its base a drinking fountain and fieldstone trough (now used as a planter).

The Parker Statue was the work of English-born American public sculptor Henry Hudson Kitson, who was also responsible for pieces at the Vicksburg National Military Park and in Boston, Salem, Plymouth, and Watertown, Massachusetts. It shows its subject holding a musket (but, unlike Daniel Chester French's Minute Man in Concord, without plow), facing east toward Boston, as if keeping watch for the king's troops. The memorial was unveiled on April 19, 1900 (the one hundred and twenty-fifth anniversary of the Lexington Fight), by a descendant of Captain Parker. Although it is frequently referred to as the "Lexington Minute Man Statue," this is something of a misnomer, perpetuated only because it has been so long in use. As historians of the Revolution and the town's well-trained guides are careful to explain, Lexington had militiamen but no minute company in 1775.

Behind the Hayes Memorial Fountain, there is a marker (the **Granite Pulpit**) on the site of Lexington's first three church buildings, including the meeting house that stood on April 19, 1775. In the center of the Green stands a memorial flagpole placed by the Lexington Bicentennial Corporation on the two hundredth anniversary of the Lexington Fight. Along the Massachusetts Avenue side of the Green, a tablet marks the location of the town's belfry in 1775. West from the Granite Pulpit, on Massachusetts Avenue about three-quarters of the way down the Common, the visitor will come to an obelisk dedicated in 1799 in memory of those who died on the Battle Green.

Revolutionary War Monument In 1799, twenty-four years after the Lexington Fight, the town erected a commemorative stone monument on the Battle Green to honor the eight men who died here on April 19, 1775. The Commonwealth of Massachusetts funded the memorial. The Reverend Jonas Clarke—minister in Lexington from 1755 to 1805, Revolutionary patriot, and host of Samuel Adams and John Hancock on the night of April 18, 1775—wrote the rousing inscription for the monument, which was placed on the site of the town's first schoolhouse. Of the eight men who died, seven were from Lexington (Robert Munroe, Jonas Parker, Samuel Hadley, Jonathan Harrington, Jr., Isaac Muzzy, Caleb Harrington, and John Brown), one from Woburn (Asahel Porter). On April 20, 1835, the remains of the Lexington men were moved from their common grave in the town's Old Burying Ground to a tomb behind the monument on the Green, with accompanying ceremonies that featured a two-hour speech by renowned orator Edward Everett. Over the two hundred-plus years since the monument was placed, it has served as the setting for many town ceremonies, including the public welcome for Lafayette in 1824, farewells to local men bound to fight in other parts of the world, and many Patriots' Day celebrations.

Revolutionary Monument, *from Concord and Lexington: The Best Collection of Views . . . (Boston: The Worcester Press, 1908), by E. F. Worcester*

Jonathan Harrington House Beyond the Battle Monument, Harrington Road runs between Massachusetts Avenue and Bedford Street, along one side of the triangular Common. At the corner of Harrington and Bedford, at 1 Harrington Road, stands the house where militiaman Jonathan Harrington, Jr., lived in 1775. From here, Mrs. Harrington observed the Lexington Fight. Wounded by British fire, her husband crawled to the steps of this house and died at her feet—a drama reenacted in Lexington each Patriots' Day.

In the 1820s, the place was home to shoemaker John Augustus. Later, it housed the clock manufactory of Burr & Chittenden. This private house, which the First Parish in Lexington has used as a rectory, is not open to the public.

Parker Boulder Heading down the Bedford Street side of the Battle Green in the direction of Lexington Center, the visitor will come upon a boulder placed near the northeast corner of the Green, where the Lexington militiamen established their line of defense on April 19, 1775. The stone marker is inscribed with Captain John Parker's exhortation to his men as the British approached.

John Parker's tablet [Parker Boulder],
from early 20th century slide lecture by Mayo Tolman

The Buckman Tavern, where members of Lexington's militia company waited for the arrival of the British troops before reassembling on the Green, stands across Bedford Street from the corner of the Common where the Minute Man Statue is located, just at the point where Bedford Street runs into Massachusetts Avenue.

Buckman Tavern Although the events of April 19, 1775, eclipse all others during the long life of the Buckman Tavern, they comprise just one brief moment in its history. The original tavern building was erected by Benjamin Muzzey, who was first licensed to keep a public house in 1693. The oldest part of the building now standing is believed to date from around 1710.

From the mid-nineteenth century, the railroad offered a faster, more efficient alternative to animal-powered transportation. Before that time, as a stop along the roads traveled by drovers moving sheep and cattle from New England points north and west, by teamsters hauling produce and merchandise, and by passenger stagecoaches, Lexington had some dozen taverns. These provided a warm fire, meals, drink (rum, hot toddy, flip, and hard cider), beds for overnight guests, feed and stable accommodations for horses, and (where there was sufficient

Buckman Tavern,
from early 20th century postcard

surrounding acreage) pasturage for animals on their way to market. (Established in 1775 to supply the Continental Army, the Brighton meat market was the destination of many drovers and herds passing through Lexington in the late eighteenth century, into the nineteenth.) The centrally-located Buckman Tavern was among the most active of Lexington's public houses. It attracted the types of patronage that other similar establishments drew, plus one more that its particular situation encouraged. Local churchgoers frequented the tavern to take their "nooning" on Sundays, warming and refreshing themselves midway through the long worship services.

This busy tavern passed from Benjamin Muzzey to his son John. On April 19, 1775, it was kept by John Buckman, whose wife was John Muzzey's granddaughter. Buckman was a member of Lexington's militia, and under his ownership the tavern benefited from the business his comrades-in-arms brought his way on training days. On the morning of the Lexington Fight, the local militia gathered on the Common and were subsequently dismissed until the British finally made their appearance. Some of these Lexington men waited in the tavern. When the regulars at last approached, the militia mustered a second time. With confrontation imminent, John Lowell (John Hancock's secretary) and

Paul Revere made an eleventh-hour foray into the Buckman Tavern to haul away a trunk of Provincial Congress documents that would have provided British authorities with much incriminating evidence had it been left behind.

John Buckman died in 1792, and Joshua Simonds acquired his public house. In 1794, Simonds sold it to his son-in-law Rufus Merriam. During Merriam's ownership, the tavern drew a more upscale clientele. While the number of drovers and teamsters seeking overnight shelter declined, other customers used the proprietor's facilities and services for dining, parties, and dances. When Merriam became Lexington's first postmaster in 1812, he constructed an ell to house the town's post office. He was the last tavern-keeper in the old structure.

The Buckman Tavern building eventually passed into the Stetson family through the marriage of Merriam's daughter Julia Ann, who married the Reverend Caleb Stetson in 1827. When the centennial anniversary of the Lexington and Concord Fights approached, Lexington asked Thomas Merriam Stetson (son of Caleb and Julia, and a lawyer in New Bedford) to serve as President of the Day. In that capacity, Stetson opened the ceremonies on the Common, where large tents were placed. He later delivered brief remarks in the dinner tent and introduced President Ulysses S. Grant. He also escorted distinguished visitors to the Buckman Tavern to warm up on the uncooperatively cold day.

In 1913, at the initiative of and with financial support from the Lexington Historical Society, the Town of Lexington purchased the Buckman Tavern and surrounding property. The building was restored by the Lexington Historical Society, which, through a lease arrangement with the town, manages the building and provides historical interpretation on site. The Buckman Tavern was made a National Historic Landmark in 1961.

Guided tours of the Buckman Tavern begin with an orientation talk in the ell. From there, visitors take in the downstairs rooms—tap room, kitchen, landlord's bedroom, and ladies' parlor. Muskets and barroom paraphernalia (flip mugs, loggerheads, and bottles) are on display, as is the old front door bearing a hole made by a musket ball on the morning of April 19, 1775. (The upstairs rooms where overnight guests stayed do not form part of the tour.)

The tavern is open to the public daily early spring through fall. Prescheduled group tours may be arranged year-round. To schedule a tour, call the Buckman Tavern at (781) 862-5598. Information about hours, fees, the museum store, Lexington Historical Society events and programs, research services, and other Lexington sites is accessible on the Lexington Historical Society homepage (http://www.lexington history.org) and on its page for historic sites (http://www.lexingtonhis-tory.org/historic-sites.html).

On Massachusetts Avenue at the Buckman Tavern, a marker to honor Prince Estabrook was placed in 2008. Estabrook—a slave who lived in Lexington and a member of the town's militia—was present on the Battle Green on April 19, 1775. This black soldier of the Revolution was wounded in the Lexington Fight. Behind the Buckman Tavern, near the Visitor Center, stands a memorial to those who have served on the ships named U.S.S. *Lexington*. Nearby is the town's World War II monument. To the left of the tavern (as the visitor faces it) is located a memorial to the Lexington "minute men" of 1775—a bronze bas relief sculpted by Bashka Paeff and dedicated on April 19, 1949.

Hancock-Clarke House To reach the Hancock-Clarke House from the Buckman Tavern, head down Hancock Street, which branches off Bedford Street just west of the tavern. The house is located at 36 Hancock Street, about a quarter of a mile from the tavern, on the visitor's left. The oldest part of it was built by Lexington's second minister, John Hancock—grandfather of John Hancock the Revolutionary leader (president of the Second Continental Congress, first governor of the Commonwealth of Massachusetts, and a signer of the Declaration of Independence).

The Reverend John Hancock succeeded Benjamin Estabrook as minister of Lexington in 1698, and put up a small parsonage. In the 1730s, his son Thomas—a wealthy Boston merchant and the uncle and benefactor of John Hancock of Revolutionary fame— enlarged the house considerably. After he lost his father in 1744, the parson's grandson John made his home here for a time, and was later a frequent visitor.

The Reverend John Hancock died in 1752. In 1755, Jonas Clarke became the minister of the First Parish. He boarded in the home of his predecessor's widow, and in 1757 married Lucy Bowes, the Reverend Hancock's granddaughter. After the Widow Hancock's death in 1760, Clarke bought the house from Thomas Hancock. Clarke lived here until his death in 1805. The house was occupied by his two unmarried daughters until 1843.

In an 1841 letter to her niece, Jonas Clarke's daughter Betty—one of twelve children—characterized her father as "a superior *Wigg* [Whig], superior minister, a Highly respectable Man, uncommon in his intellectual faculties and, above all, a *Christian,* who served his Lord and Master, was faithfull to his People, gave his strength to labour for his Family, his hours of Rest to his pen so that his People's souls should not be neglected." The dignified Clarke was an inspiring preacher. In his sermons, he suggested Biblical parallels to the situation of the American colonists in the 1770s, thereby reinforcing their determination to defend their rights and liberties. Moreover, he did not shrink from direct political involvement. In the 1760s and 1770s, he prepared written instructions for Lexington's representatives to the Great and General Court in Boston as they responded to the growing tension between the colonies and the mother country.

Hancock-Clark [Clarke] House, *from Concord and Lexington: The Best Collection of Views . . . (Boston: The Worcester Press, 1908), by E. F. Worcester*

Having attended the Provincial Congress in Concord, John Hancock and Samuel Adams were Clarke's houseguests on the night of April 18, 1775, as was Dorothy Quincy, Hancock's fiancée. Dr. Joseph Warren of Boston sent Paul Revere and William Dawes to Lexington to warn Hancock and Adams of the British approach. They arrived separately at the parsonage around midnight, delivered their message, and rode on toward Concord. After his capture and brief detention by a British patrol, Revere returned to the house, where Hancock and Adams remained in protracted discussion. (Hancock wanted to stay in Lexington, Adams to leave.) Revere herded them along to safer haven.

After the Lexington Fight, the Reverend Clarke went to the meeting house to pray over the bodies of the eight men—seven of them his parishioners—who had been killed in the gunfire on the Common that morning. Their makeshift wooden coffins were loaded onto carts, drawn to the nearby cemetery, and buried in a hastily-dug common grave. Clarke, his wife, and two of his children were present at the burial. Fearing that the British would discover and desecrate the bodies, Clarke urged covering the raw earth of the new grave with boughs. In 1799, he wrote the inscription for the monument on the Battle Green to honor these Lexington heroes, whose remains were moved in 1835 to a more visible final resting place behind that memorial.

The Hancock-Clarke House was open to visitors during the centennial celebration of the Lexington Fight on April 19, 1875. Twenty-one years later, in 1896, the Lexington Historical Society stepped up when it became clear that the house was to be demolished. The owner at the time was willing to sell the building, but only for removal to another site. The society purchased it and also a lot on the other side of Hancock Street, moved the building to the new site, restored it, and opened it to the public in June 1898. In 1971, the house was added to the National Register of Historic Places and designated a National Historic Landmark. In 1974, in anticipation of the bicentennial of the Lexington Fight, the Lexington Historical Society moved the Hancock-Clarke House back across Hancock Street to its original site, onto a new foundation, incorporating into the basement a climate-controlled archival facility for document storage. In 2009, the house celebrated its reopening after a year-long restoration project that provided major structural repair.

Guides in period dress take visitors through the house and tell the stories behind the furnishings, personal effects, and portraits of the two families who once lived here. Also displayed at this site are William Diamond's drum and Major Pitcairn's pistols—iconic artifacts of April 19, 1775, owned by the Lexington Historical Society. In addition, since 1991, the society has maintained a Fire Equipment Museum in the barn behind the house.

The house is open to the public early spring through fall. There is a parking area behind it. Access to the house is by admission fee. Group tours must be scheduled in advance. To make reservations for a group tour, call (781) 862-0295. An interpretive film is offered in the entrance area. For more information, call the Lexington Historical Society office at (781) 862-1703, or visit the society's historic sites Web page at http://www.lexingtonhistory.org/explore-lexington.html.

Having toured the Hancock-Clarke House, visitors ready to see more of Lexington's Revolutionary sites should backtrack down Hancock Street to the Battle Green.

Old Burying Ground The access path to Lexington's Old Burying Ground is located along Massachusetts Avenue, just beyond Harrington Road, a short distance west of the Common. This cemetery consists of land acquired by the town in several parcels over time. The oldest gravestones in it date from 1690. The Reverends John Hancock and Jonas Clarke lie in rest here. On April 19, 1775, the eight Colonial men killed on the Green were buried in this cemetery, in a trench "as near the Woods as possible," as the Reverend Clarke's daughter Betty wrote, camouflaged with brush. (Their remains were moved to the Battle Green in 1835 and reinterred with solemn ceremony.) A British soldier who was wounded on the retreat from Concord and died three days later at the Buckman Tavern was buried in an unmarked grave in the Old Burying Ground. In 1905, the Lexington Historical Society erected a marker on the site of his grave. A monument to Captain John Parker was placed in the cemetery in 1884.

Visitors interested in social history as well as in the story of the Lexington Fight will enjoy walking among the graves and reading epitaphs in this classic New England cemetery.

Belfry Hill Lexington's 1775 meeting house had no bell tower. A freestanding belfry called the people of the town to church, knelled for the dead, and signaled other events in local life. The original belfry was placed on what is now known as Belfry Hill, which is located on Massachusetts Avenue almost directly across from the Lexington Minute Man Statue on the Common. The short pathway to the reconstructed belfry at the top of the hill is well-marked from the street, but the footing is somewhat rough and requires care on the ascent and descent. A marker on the belfry at the top traces the history of this structure: "This belfry was erected on this hill in 1761 and removed to the Common in 1768. In it was hung the bell which rung out the alarm on the 19th of April 1775. In 1797 it was removed to the Parker homestead in the south part of the town. In 1891 it was brought back to this hill by the Lexington Historical Society. Destroyed by a gale 1909, rebuilt 1910."

Reconstructed belfry on Belfry Hill, *from Concord and Lexington: The Best Collection of Views . . . (Boston: The Worcester Press, 1908), by E. F. Worcester*

Cary Memorial Hall The Isaac Harris Cary Memorial Hall is at the easternmost end of Lexington's business district, on the same side of Massachusetts Avenue as the Buckman Tavern and the Visitor Center. It is located at 1605 Massachusetts Avenue, between the Lexington town offices and police station. The hall provides event facilities and a large auditorium for community concerts, performances, lectures, programs, and meetings. (For more information, visit the Web pages at http://www.caryhalllexington.com and—regarding building rental—http://www.lexingtonma.gov/facility-rental.)

Cary Memorial Hall houses several works of art commemorating the Lexington Fight. Henry Sandham's large painting *The Dawn of Liberty* (owned by the Lexington Historical Society) dominates the entrance hall. To its left and right are marble statues of Samuel Adams and John Hancock, commissioned by the local committee charged with planning Lexington's 1875 centennial celebration. In 1873, the committee engaged two American artists in Italy—Martin Milmore in Rome and Thomas Ridgeway Gould in Florence—to sculpt the statues. The finished works were delivered to Lexington in time for the ceremonies of April 19, 1875, and were unveiled in the pavilion tent on the Green. Gould's statue of Hancock stands to the right of *The Dawn of Liberty,* Milmore's statue of Adams to the left.

The intersection of Woburn Street and Massachusetts Avenue lies just beyond Cary Memorial Hall. (Woburn Street runs to the left, Massachusetts Avenue to the right.) To reach the Munroe Tavern from the center of Lexington, continue east down Massachusetts Avenue. On the left, a short distance past the intersection, a stone cannon marks the spot where Earl Percy placed one of two field pieces sent to Lexington along with the reinforcements—a thousand men—requested on the morning of April 19, 1775, by Lieutenant Colonel Francis Smith. The cannon protected the retreating regulars that afternoon. The Munroe Tavern stands some distance farther along Massachusetts Avenue, on the right-hand side.

Munroe Tavern The Munroe Tavern at 1332 Massachusetts Avenue has significance in relation to the story of April 19, 1775, to Lexington's local history, and—as a fine example of a public house that operated in the seventeenth, eighteenth, and nineteenth centuries—to New England social history. The original part of the structure as it survives was built in the late seventeenth century by William Munroe, a son of William Munro (the name has several variant spellings), the first member of the family in Lexington. Munro the progenitor—a Scottish prisoner of war captured at the Battle of Worcester and exiled to America—was indentured to cover the cost of his transport to the New World. Having served the term of his indenture, around 1660 he settled in Cambridge Farms (Lexington's name prior to its incorporation as a separate town), and became a prosperous and active community member. His son William (one of Munro's thirteen children by two wives) built the tavern in 1695. The following year, he was licensed to keep a public house.

The tavern passed into the Comee (Comey) family through the marriage of a daughter of the second William. It was sold out of the family in 1730. In 1770, Colonel William Munroe—great-grandson of the first William—bought it from John Buckman (keeper of the Buckman Tavern in the center of town in April of 1775). This William—orderly sergeant of the Lexington militia company—ran the tavern from 1770 and was its proprietor on April 19, 1775. He died in 1827. His son Jonas ran the place during the final decade of his father's life.

Under the ownership of the Revolutionary William, the tavern building was considerably enlarged. He added the back part of the structure and, later, an ell, the lower level of which housed a store, the upper level a large room that served as a dancehall and also as the meeting place of Lexington's Hiram Lodge of Freemasons. (The ell was taken down about 1850.) Jonas Munroe kept the tavern until 1858, by which time the railroad had put a serious dent in his business. He died in 1860. The Lexington Historical Society acquired the Munroe Tavern in 1911 as a bequest from James S. Munroe, one of Jonas's sons. It was listed on the National Register of Historic Places in 1976.

Munroe Tavern, from early 20th century postcard

Most Colonial tradesmen and service providers were farmers in addition to whatever other occupations they pursued, and Colonel William Munroe was no exception. He maintained a farm as well as a tavern. Located a mile from the Common, his farm was sizeable, and in this he had an advantage over those who kept public houses closer to the town center. In the period when drovers from New Hampshire and Vermont regularly passed through Lexington on their way to Brighton or Boston, it took considerable land to accommodate herds of cattle and droves of sheep staying for a day or two at a time. This clientele formed a significant part of Munroe's business.

As orderly sergeant of the Lexington militia, Colonel William Munroe was away from his home and place of business on the night of April 18, 1775, and during the following day. Late in the afternoon of April 18, he responded to the report of a local man who, on his return from market, had observed armed British soldiers in the vicinity. Munroe assembled the militia, selected eight men to guard Hancock and Adams at the Reverend Clarke's house, and remained there with them. After Paul Revere arrived, Munroe dispatched a rider to confirm Revere's report of the British approach. (That rider was taken by a British advance patrol, as were a second and third sent on the same mission, which was finally accomplished by a fourth man whose horse shied and halted in its tracks, giving its rider opportunity to spot the oncoming troops and to turn back.) On the morning of April 19, Munroe stood with his comrades on the Green. Later, he participated in the pursuit of the British on their way back from Concord. Meanwhile, as the events of that day unfolded, his frightened wife fled to the woods with their three children.

Earl Percy was in charge of the relief column that assisted the British expeditionary force on its return from Concord. He used the Munroe Tavern as his headquarters for a period of an hour and a half on the afternoon of April 19. The dining room was used as a field hospital. The tavern was overrun by the British, who helped themselves to food and drink, sacked the place, killed John Raymond (left to mind the place in Munroe's absence), and set the building on fire as they departed (the fire was put out). With his reinforcements, Earl Percy subsequently led the depleted and dispirited British troops back to Boston from Lexington.

When George Washington came to Lexington in November 1789, he visited the Battle Green and dined at the Munroe Tavern. An elm tree then standing in front of the house provided a perch from which local boys tried to catch a glimpse of the great man. In the upstairs tavern room where Washington was entertained, visitors today may view the table at which he sat and objects and documents associated with his visit.

The Munroe Tavern is accessible by admission fee. Guided tours begin in an orientation area that was once the tavern's kitchen, and proceed through both the downstairs and upstairs rooms. Tour guides focus on the ownership and the history and uses of the tavern building, the story of the Munroe family, the original furniture and artifacts on the site, George Washington's visit here, and the lives and perspective of British soldiers in 1775 (this last a recently adopted emphasis). There is a period garden outside the entry to the house. The tavern is open from early spring into the fall. Group tours must be prescheduled. There is free parking for those who arrive by car, and bus service to the tavern from Depot Square. For more information, call the Lexington Historical Society office at (781) 862-1703, or visit the society's historic sites Web page at http://www.lexingtonhistory.org/historic-sites.html. To make reservations for a group tour, call (781) 862-0295.

Scottish Rite Masonic Museum & Library The Scottish Rite Masonic Museum & Library is a good place to wrap up a tour of Lexington or Concord, or to spend a few leisurely hours on a separate excursion. Established by the Scottish Rite Masons of the Northern Masonic Jurisdiction of the United States to honor the signers of the Declaration of Independence, it was a bicentennial project, dedicated in 1975. It was originally known as the Museum of Our National Heritage, later as the National Heritage Museum.

The museum is located at 33 Marrett Road (a part of Route 2A) in Lexington, at the intersection of Massachusetts Avenue and 2A. To reach it from the center of Lexington, go east on Massachusetts Avenue, past the Munroe Tavern, and make a hard right onto Marrett Road, then another right into the museum's parking lot. If coming from Concord, drive east on 2A and take a left at the museum entrance. From I-95/128, take Exit 30A onto Route 2A East. The museum will be on the left about three miles from the exit. From Route 495, take Route 2 East to Exit 55 and turn left onto Pleasant Street. After half a mile, Pleasant Street merges into Routes 4 and 225, following which brings the visitor to Massachusetts Avenue. Turn left off Massachusetts Avenue onto Marrett Road, and then right at the museum entrance. From the Massachusetts Turnpike, take I-95/128 North, get off at Exit 30A, head east on 2A, and travel three miles to the museum entrance (on the left). To reach the museum by public transportation from Boston or Cambridge, take the Red Line to Alewife Station, then Bus 62 or 76.

The Scottish Rite Masonic Museum & Library holds collections (including library and archival materials) relating to the history of Freemasonry in the context of American history and culture. It features changing exhibits, with a focus on local Revolutionary history, and offers a variety of programs and workshops. Admission and parking are free of charge. The museum is handicapped accessible, and has a café, gift shop, and restroom facilities. Self-guided and guided tours are available. (Group tours should be scheduled in advance.) The museum is open Wednesday through Saturday. It is closed on Thanksgiving, Christmas Eve and Christmas Day, and New Year's Day. The museum's Van Gordon-Williams Library and Archives are also open Wednesday through Saturday.

The Scottish Rite Masonic Museum & Library maintains an informative, engaging website at http://www.monh.org. The phone number is (781) 861-6559. To make reservations for a group visit, call (781) 457-4142. To contact the Van Gordon-Williams Library and Archives, call (781) 457-4125.

On to Concord Those who tour Concord after seeing Lexington can reach Monument Square—the best place to begin a Concord visit—by traveling along the Battle Road (Route 2A) from Lexington through Lincoln, possibly stopping at one or more of the sites along the way—Fiske Hill, the Minute Man Visitor Center of the Minute Man National Historical Park, Bloody Angle, the Paul Revere Capture Site, and the Hartwell Tavern. Past these landmarks, turn right off 2A onto Lexington Road, which leads into and ends at Monument Square.

SUGGESTED ITINERARIES

If you have half a day to spend . . .

A free half-day is insufficient to visit both Lexington and Concord except in the most cursory way. If you cannot spare more time, it's best to choose which town you'd most like to visit and to save the other for another trip. Be sure to check ahead for the hours of the various sites so that you don't waste precious minutes discovering that you can't see what you had planned to see.

If you opt to spend half a day in Lexington, you can see quite a lot by focusing on the center of town—the **Buckman Tavern**, the monuments on the **Battle Green**, the **Hancock-Clarke House**, the **Old Burying Ground**, and **Belfry Hill**, all of which are in walking distance of one another.

If Concord is your preference, the process of narrowing down a half-day itinerary is complicated by the number and dispersion of historical sites. In the course of three or four hours, a visitor can comfortably take in **Orchard House**, the **Concord Museum**, and one other site (perhaps the **Emerson House**, **The Wayside**, the **Hill Burying Ground**, or—at some distance away—the **Old Manse** and **North Bridge**). Those with a particular interest in the American Revolution may prefer to start out at the North Bridge, proceed to the Old Manse, stop at the Hill Burying Ground, and conclude at the Concord Museum and/or one of the several historic houses in its vicinity. Thoreauvians will want to focus on **Walden Pond**, and can easily spend two or three hours there. Time and transportation permitting, they may also want to drive by the **Thoreau Birthplace** on Virginia Road and the **Thoreau-Alcott House** on Main Street.

The town centers of both Lexington and Concord offer a number of eateries, both formal and informal. Whichever town you decide to explore, you may want to plan on preceding or following your half-day tour with some sort of refreshment. The Visitor Center in each town can provide recommendations for a variety of tastes and pocketbooks.

If you have a whole day . . .

A whole day will accommodate a more intensive focus on the historic sites of either Lexington or Concord or a combined tour of some of the sites of each. Those who want to see Lexington in greater depth can follow the itinerary for a half-day there, adding—perhaps after a stop at the **Lexington Visitors Center** and lunch downtown—a visit to the **Munroe Tavern,** and the **Scottish Rite Masonic Museum & Library.** (**Cary Memorial Hall** is a quick stop on the way to the Munroe Tavern.) Those who want to see more of Concord can start at **Orchard House,** then take in **The Wayside** or the **Emerson House** and the **Concord Museum** before exploring **Monument Square,** from which it's easy to find both the **Concord Visitor Center** and places for lunch. The afternoon might include a visit to the **South Burying Ground** and the **Concord Free Public Library,** followed by a trek to Monument Street (via Monument Square) to see the **Old Manse** and the **North Bridge,** or by a tour of **Sleepy Hollow Cemetery.** There may even be enough time to take in **Thoreau's Cove at Walden Pond.** (In warm weather, travelers with children should consider a family swim.)

Those who want to sample the sights of both Lexington and Concord will require transportation between the two—a car or the regularly-scheduled Liberty Ride. Start in either town, plan on a mid-day break for travel (maybe including a stop at the **Minute Man Visitor Center** on Route 2A) and lunch, and follow the half-day itinerary for each town.

If you have two days . . .

The tourist with two full days to devote to Lexington and Concord has time enough to see the major historic sights of the area. The obvious division of time is one day in each of the towns, following the whole-day itineraries outlined above. If you want to see more of Concord than of Lexington, follow the half-day itinerary for Lexington and give Concord a day and a half. The half-day in Concord could be spent at **Orchard House,** the **Concord Museum,** and **The Wayside** or **Emerson House** (both, if scheduling permits). The full day might include the **North Bridge,** the **Old Manse,** and **Monument Square** before lunch, and after lunch **Concord Art,** the **Concord Free Public Library,** a glimpse of several of the historic structures in the neighborhood of the library, and a walk through **Sleepy Hollow Cemetery,** a trip to **Walden Pond,** or a boat trip from the **South Bridge Boat House.**

If you have three days . . .
A three-day sojourn will allow the visitor to see everything in the two-day itinerary (all of Lexington's major sites and a number of Concord's, including both **Walden Pond** and **Sleepy Hollow Cemetery**), plus some of the other Concord sights located beyond the center of town. Those who can't get enough history may choose to visit the Colonel James **Barrett Farm** or **Meriam's Corner**. The more literary-minded may prefer the **Thoreau Birthplace**. Those drawn to the natural world might enjoy walking in the **Estabrook Woods** or the **Great Meadows National Wildlife Refuge** or boating on the **Sudbury River**. But map out your course ahead of time—too much backtracking will cut into the time available for meaningful sightseeing. It may be better to pick one of the major roads described in this guidebook—**Lowell Road** or **Main Street** or **Lexington Road**, for example—and to follow it as far as time allows than to seek out sites located along multiple routes.

If you are planning an extended stay . . .
The visitor lucky enough to have four, five, or more days in the area should be able to take in all of the historic sites of Lexington and all Concord sites of possible interest, including **West Concord** and **Nine Acre Corner**. Blessed with abundant time, you may even allow yourself to visit the several area bakeries to compare the coffee and treats sold by each; to linger over the local newspaper at breakfast or lunch; to attend a service in a Lexington or Concord house of worship; or to view the artwork or check your e-mail at the **Concord Free Public Library**. And if you need a change of pace, Cambridge and Boston are readily accessible by Commuter Rail. But whether your stay is compressed or leisurely, be aware that the proud and knowledgeable people of Lexington and Concord are generally eager to answer visitors' questions, if they can.

CONTACT INFORMATION
for Concord and Lexington Historic Sites and Organizations

With the single exception of the South Bridge Boat House, this listing excludes businesses. Information about lodging, restaurants, stores, and services in Concord and Lexington is available through the Chamber of Commerce and Visitor Center in each town.

Concord

Bruce Freeman Rail Trail
Friends of the Bruce Freeman
   Rail Trail
P.O. Box 1192
Concord, Massachusetts 01742
www.brucefreemanrailtrail.org

Concord (Town of)

   Cemetery Division
   (978) 318-3233
   www.concordma.gov/pages/
      ConcordMA_Cemetery/index

   Historic Districts Commission
   141 Keyes Road, First Floor
   Concord, Massachusetts 01742
   (978) 318-3299
   Fax: (978) 318-3291
   www.concordma.gov/pages/
      ConcordMA_HDC/index

   Historical Commission
   141 Keyes Road, First Floor
   Concord, Massachusetts 01742
   (978) 318-3290
   Fax: (978) 318-3291
   www.concordma.gov/pages/
      ConcordMA_HistComm/index

   Division of Natural Resources
   141 Keyes Road
   Concord, Massachusetts 01742
   (978) 318-3285
   Fax: (978) 318-3291
   www.concordma.gov/pages/
      ConcordMA_NaturalResources/
      index
   *Guidelines for use of town
      conservation land:*
   http://www.concordma.gov/pages/
      ConcordMA_Natural
      Resources/conservationland/
      consland

   Town Clerk
   22 Monument Square
   P.O. Box 535
   Concord, Massachusetts 01742
   (978) 318-3080
   Fax: (978) 318-3093
   www.concordma.gov/pages/
      ConcordMA_TownClerk/index
   E-mail contact: TownClerk@
      concordma.gov

Concord Art
37 Lexington Rd
Concord, Massachusetts 01742
(978) 369-2578
www.concordart.org

Concord Chamber of Commerce
15 Walden St., Suite 7
Concord, Massachusetts 01742
(978) 369-3120
Fax: (978) 369-1515
www.concordchamberofcommerce.org

Concord Free Public Library
129 Main Street
Concord, Massachusetts 01742
Circulation: (978) 318-3301;
    Reference: (978) 318-3347
Fax: (978) 318-3344
www.concordlibrary.org

William Munroe Special Collections
(978) 318-3342
www.concordlibrary.org/scollect/
    scoll.html

Concord Historical Collaborative
(Formed for joint programming by a
number of local historical sites and
agencies): Contact any of Concord's
historical sites for more information.

Concord Museum
Cambridge Turnpike at Lexington
    Road
Concord, Massachusetts 01742
(978) 369-9763
Taped information: (978) 369-9609
www.concordmuseum.org
E-mail contact: cm1@concord
    museum.org

Concord Visitor Center
58 Main Street
Concord, Massachusetts 01742
(978) 368-3120
www.concordchamberofcommerce.
    org/visitor-information/

Emerson House
28 Cambridge Turnpike
Concord, Massachusetts 01742
(978) 369-2236

Great Meadows National Wildlife
Refuge
Concord Unit
Monsen Road
Concord, Massachusetts 01742

Sudbury Unit
73 Weir Hill Road
Sudbury, MA 01776
(978) 443-4661
Fax: (978) 443-2898
http://www.fws.gov/refuge/great_
    meadows/
E-mail contact: fw5rw_emnwr@fws.
    gov

MBTA Commuter Rail (Fitchburg/
South Acton line)
www.mbta.com/schedules_and_
    maps/rail/lines/?route=FITCHBRG

Minute Man National
Historical Park
Minute Man Visitor Center
250 North Great Road (Route 2A)
Lincoln, Massachusetts 01773
(Note: Use North Bridge Visitor
    Center address for mail.)
(781) 674-1920
www.nps.gov/mima/index.htm

North Bridge Visitor Center
174 Liberty Street
Concord, Massachusetts 01742
Main number: (978) 369-6993
Front desk: (978) 318-7810
www.nps.gov/mima/index.htm

The Wayside
455 Lexington Road
Concord, Massachusetts 01742
(Note: Use North Bridge Visitor
    Center address for mail.)
(978) 369-6993
www.nps.gov/mima/index.htm

Barrett Farm
Street address: 448 Barrett's Mill
    Road
Concord, Massachusetts 01742
Administrative address: Minute Man
    National Historical Park
174 Liberty Street
Concord, Massachusetts 01742
(978) 369-6993
www.jamesbarrettfarm.org/

Old Manse
269 Monument Street
Concord, Massachusetts 01742
(978) 369-3909
http://www.thetrustees.org/places-
    to-visit/greater-boston/old-manse.
    html
E-mail contact: oldmanse@ttor.org

The Robbins House
320 Monument Street
P.O. Box 506
Concord, Massachusetts 01742
(978) 254-1745
www.robbinshouse.org
E-mail contact: info@robbinshouse.
    org

Louisa May Alcott's Orchard House
399 Lexington Road
P.O. Box 343
Concord, Massachusetts 01742
(978) 369-4118
Fax: (978) 369-1367
www.louisamayalcott.org
E-mail contact: info@louisamay
    alcott.org

Save Our Heritage
57 Main Street
Concord, Massachusetts 01742
(978) 369-6662
www.saveourheritage.com

South Bridge Boat House
496 Main Street
Concord, Massachusetts 01742
(978) 369-9438
River cruise and catering informa-
    tion: (978) 371-1785
www.southbridgeboathouse.com

Thoreau Farm (Thoreau Birthplace)
341 Virginia Road
P.O. Box 454
Concord, Massachusetts 01742
(978) 451-0300
www.thoreaufarm.org/
E-mail contact: info@thoreaufarm.
    org

Thoreau Society
341 Virginia Road
Concord, Massachusetts 01742
Office: (978) 369-5310
www.thoreausociety.org
Shop at Walden Pond:
    915 Walden Street
    Concord, Massachusetts 01742
    (978) 287-5477
    www.thoreausociety.org/about/
    shop-walden
Collections: (781) 259-4730;
    www.walden.org/library

Walden Pond State Reservation
915 Walden Street
Concord, Massachusetts 01742
(978) 369-3254
http://www.mass.gov/eea/agencies/
    dcr/massparks/region-north/
    walden-pond-state-reservation.
    html

Lexington

Lexington (Town of)
Cary Memorial Hall
1605 Massachusetts Avenue
Lexington, Massachusetts 02420
http://www.caryhalllexington.com
and http://www.lexingtonma.gov/
facility-rental
Rental inquiries: (781) 274-8904

Historic Districts Commission
1625 Massachusetts Avenue
Lexington, Massachusetts 02420
(781) 698-4524
www.lexingtonma.gov/historic-
districts-commission

Historical Commission
1625 Massachusetts Avenue
Lexington, Massachusetts 02420
(781) 698-4525
www.lexingtonma.gov/historical-
commission

Lexpress Bus Service
Lexington Community Center
39 Marrett Road
Lexington, Massachusetts 02421
(781) 861-1210
www.lexingtonma.gov/lexpress

Tourism Committee
1625 Massachusetts Avenue
Lexington, Massachusetts 02420
www.lexingtonma.gov/tourism-
committee

Town Clerk
1625 Massachusetts Avenue
Lexington, Massachusetts 02420
(781) 698-4550
Fax: (781) 861-2754
http://www.lexingtonma.gov/town-
clerk

Lexington Bicycle Routes
See links from
http://www.lexingtonma.gov/
bicycle-advisory-committee

Lexington Chamber of Commerce
1875 Massachusetts Ave
Lexington, Massachusetts 02420
(781) 862-2480
www.lexingtonchamber.org/
E-mail contact: director@lexington
chamber.org

Lexington Historical Society
P.O. Box 514
Lexington, Massachusetts 02420
(781) 862-1703
Group tour reservations:
(781) 862-0295
www.lexingtonhistory.org/
E-mail contacts:
office@lexingtonhistory.org;
tours@lexingtonhistory.org;
director@lexingtonhistory.org;
collections@lexingtonhistory.org

Buckman Tavern
1 Bedford Street
Lexington, Massachusetts 02420
(781) 862-5598
www.lexingtonhistory.org/historic-
sites.html

Hancock-Clarke House
36 Hancock Street
Lexington, Massachusetts 02420
(781) 861-0928
www.lexingtonhistory.org/historic-
sites.html

Munroe Tavern
1332 Massachusetts Avenue
Lexington, Massachusetts 02420
(781) 862-0295
www.lexingtonhistory.org/historic-
     sites.html

Lexington Visitors Center
1875 Massachusetts Ave
Lexington, Massachusetts 02420
(781) 862-1450
http://www.lexingtonma.gov/visitors-
     center

Liberty Ride
Taped information: (781) 698-4586
www.libertyride.us/libertyride.html

MBTA Bus Service (Routes 62
and 76)
www.mbta.com/schedules_and_
     maps/bus/routes/?route=62
www.mbta.com/schedules_and_
     maps/bus/routes/?route=76

Minute Man National Historical
Park Minute Man Visitor Center
250 North Great Road (Route 2A)
Lincoln, Massachusetts 01773
(Note: Use North Bridge Visitor
     Center address for mail.)
(781) 674-1920
www.nps.gov/mima/index.htm

Scottish Rite Masonic Museum
& Library
33 Marrett Road
Lexington, Massachusetts 02421
(781) 861-6559
Reservations for group visits:
(781) 457-4142
www.monh.org

Van Gordon-Williams Library and
Archives
(781) 457-4125
www.monh.org/library-archives/

FOR FURTHER READING

THERE IS AN EXTENSIVE LITERATURE on the history and authors of Concord and on the Lexington Fight. The following list suggests some of the published sources that expand upon topics briefly presented in *Historic Concord*. It is by no means exhaustive.

In recommending writings of the Concord authors, an effort has been made to focus on readily obtainable collections, when available. A few biographies are included for each major author, but no literary criticism. There are, after all, plenty of published guides to aid the specialist in finding scholarly editions and critical resources.

Alcott, Amos Bronson. *Concord Days.* Ann Arbor: Scholarly Publishing Office, University of Michigan Library, 2007. (Reprint edition.)

————*How Like an Angel Came I Down: Conversations with Children on the Gospels.* Ed. Alice O. Howell. Herndon, Virginia: Lindisfarne Books (a division of Steiner Books), 1991.

————*The Journals of Bronson Alcott.* Ed. Odell Shepard. Boston: Little, Brown, 1938.

————*The Letters of A. Bronson Alcott.* Ed. Richard L. Herrnstadt. Ames: Iowa State University Press, 1969.

————*Notes of Conversations, 1848–1875.* Ed. Karen English. Madison, New Jersey: Fairleigh Dickinson University Press, 2007.

  About:

  Dahlstrand, Frederick C. *Amos Bronson Alcott: An Intellectual Biography.* Rutherford, New Jersey: Fairleigh Dickinson University Press, 1982.

  Peabody, Elizabeth Palmer. *Record of a School.* Carlisle, Massachusetts: Applewood Books, 2006. (Reprint of a key nineteenth-century work on Alcott's Temple School.)

  Sanborn, Franklin Benjamin, and William Torrey Harris. *A. Bronson Alcott: His Life and Philosophy.* 2 vols. Boston: Roberts Brothers, 1893.

  Shepard, Odell. *Pedlar's Progress: The Life of Bronson Alcott.* Boston: Little, Brown, 1937.

Alcott, Louisa May. *Behind a Mask: The Unknown Thrillers of Louisa May Alcott.* Ed. Madeleine Stern. New York: William Morrow & Company, 1975. (*Plots and Counterplots,* a second collection of Alcott's pseudonymous thrillers edited by Madeleine Stern, was published by Morrow in 1976.)

————*The Journals of Louisa May Alcott.* Ed. Joel Myerson and Daniel Shealy. Athens: University of Georgia Press, 1997.

————*Life, Letters, and Journals.* Ed. Ednah D. Cheney. Avenel, New Jersey: Gramercy Books, 1995. (Reprint of basic early source.)

————*Little Women.* Ed. Gregory Eiselein and Anne K. Phillips. New York: Norton, 2003.

————*Little Women Abroad: The Alcott Sisters' Letters from Europe, 1870–1871.* Ed. Daniel Shealy. Athens: University of Georgia Press, 2008.

————*Little Women, Little Men, Jo's Boys.* New York: Library of America, 2005.

————*Louisa May Alcott: Selected Fiction.* Ed. Daniel Shealy, Madeleine Stern, and Joel Myerson. Boston: Little, Brown, 1990.

————*Louisa May Alcott's Civil War.* Introd. by Jan Turnquist. Roseville, Minnesota: Edinborough Press, 2007.

————*The Selected Letters of Louisa May Alcott.* Ed. Joel Myerson and Daniel Shealy. Boston: Little, Brown, 1987.

    About:

    Bedell, Madelon. *The Alcotts: Biography of a Family.* New York: C. N. Potter, 1980.

    Matteson, John. *Eden's Outcasts: The Story of Louisa May Alcott and Her Father.* New York: Norton, 2008.

    Reisen, Harriet. *Louisa May Alcott: The Woman Behind Little Women.* New York: Henry Holt, 2009.

    Saxton, Martha. *Louisa May: A Modern Biography of Louisa May Alcott.* Boston: Houghton Mifflin, 1977. (Reprinted in 1995 by Noonday Press, New York.)

    Stern, Madeleine. *Louisa May Alcott.* Norman: University of Oklahoma Press, 1985.

Bartlett, George Bradford. *Concord Historic, Literary and Picturesque.* 16th ed., rev. Boston: Lothrop, 1895. (An enlarged version of Bartlett's *Concord Guide Book,* 1880).

Brewster, William. *Concord River: Selections from the Journals of William Brewster.* Ed. Smith O. Dexter. Cambridge: Harvard University Press, 1937.

Brooks, Paul. *The Old Manse and the People Who Lived There.* N.p.: Trustees of Reservations, 1983.

————*The People of Concord: One Year in the Flowering of New England.* Chester, Connecticut: Globe Pequot Press, 1990.

Cheever, Susan. *American Bloomsbury.* New York: Simon & Schuster, 2006. (This popular recent book is best read as a spirited personal interpretation rather than for factual detail.)

Clarke, Jonas. *The Fate of Blood-thirsty Oppressors and God's tender Care of his distressed People. A Sermon, Preached at Lexington, April 19, 1776.*

To commemorate the Murder, Bloodshed, and Commencement of Hostilities, between Great Britain and America, in that Town, by a Brigade of Troops of George III, under Command of Lieutenant-Colonel Smith, on the Nineteenth of April, 1775. To Which is Added, a Brief Narrative of the principal Transactions of that Day . . . Boston: Printed by Powars and Willis, 1776; reprint, Boston: Franklin Press; Rand, Avery, & Co., 1875.

Coburn, Frank Warren. *The Battle of April 19, 1775, in Lexington, Concord, Lincoln, Arlington, Cambridge, Somerville and Charlestown, Massachusetts.* Lexington: Published by the author, 1912. Bound with this title: Coburn, Frank Warren. *Muster Rolls of the Participating Companies of American Militia and Minute-Men in the Battle of April 19, 1775, Mostly from the Archives of the Commonwealth of Massachusetts.* Lexington: Published by the author, 1912.

Concord (Mass.). *Proceedings at the Centennial Celebration of Concord Fight, April 19, 1875.* Concord: The Town, 1876.

Concord Antiquarian Society. Pamphlets. Concord: The Society, 1901-1916. (Brief monographs on a number of Concord-related topics. Among the titles published: *The Concord Minute Men; Events of April Nineteeth; Early Town Records; "Graves and Worms and Epitaphs"; Indian Relics in Concord; John Jack, the Slave, and Daniel Bliss, the Tory; The Old Women; The Plantation at Musketequid; Preliminaries of Concord Fight; Story of an Old House; Wright's Tavern.*)

Concord Free Public Library. William Munroe Special Collections. Web pages. http://www.concordlibrary.org/scollect/scoll.html. (A rich and varied set of pages including interpretive online exhibitions, a brief history of Concord, historical photographs, oral histories, searchable nineteenth century town reports and newspapers, and much more. Bronson Alcott's reports as Concord's Superintendent of Schools are available on the town reports pages.)

Concord Historical Commission. *Survey of Historical and Architectural Resources, Concord, Massachusetts.* Rev. ed. 4 vols. Concord: The Commission, 2002.

Concord Magazine [electronic magazine]. Concord: Hometown Websmith/ Windfall, 1998-2008. http://www.concordma.com/magazine. (An online magazine containing articles on aspects of Concord history. Includes many pieces on Revolutionary topics by D. Michael Ryan, and two by Aryeh Finklestein on the grave of the British soldiers at the North Bridge. The *Concord Magazine* transformed from magazine to a blog in 2009. The Web address for the blog is http://www.concordma.com/blog/.)

Concord Museum. *The Concord Museum: Decorative Arts from a New England Collection.* Ed. David F. Wood. Concord: The Museum, 1996.

Donahue, Brian. *The Great Meadow: Farmers and the Land in Colonial Concord.* New Haven: Yale University Press, 2004.

Emerson, Ralph Waldo. *Collected Poems and Translations.* Ed. Harold Bloom and Paul Kane. New York: Library of America, 1994.

————*The Collected Works of Ralph Waldo Emerson.* Cambridge: Belknap Press of Harvard University Press, 1971-present. (The definitive scholarly edition, superseding the 1903-1904 Centenary Edition published by Houghton Mifflin.)

————*Emerson's Prose and Poetry.* Ed. Joel Porte and Saundra Morris. New York: Norton, 2001.

————*Essays & Lectures.* New York: Library of America, 1991.

————*Emerson in His Journals.* Ed. Joel Porte. Cambridge: Belkap Press of Harvard University Press, 1982.

————*A Historical Discourse, Delivered Before the Citizens of Concord, 12th September, 1835. On the Second Centennial Anniversary of the Incorporation of the Town.* Concord: G. F. Bemis, printer, 1835. (Published in 1883 in the volume titled *Miscellanies* in the Riverside Edition of Emerson's complete works.)

————*The Selected Letters of Ralph Waldo Emerson.* Ed. Joel Myerson. New York: Columbia University Press, 1997.

   About:

   Baker, Carlos. *Emerson Among the Eccentrics: A Group Portrait.* New York: Penguin Books, 1996.

   Buell, Lawrence. *Emerson.* Cambridge: Belknap Press of Harvard University Press, 2003.

   Cabot, James Elliot. *A Memoir of Ralph Waldo Emerson.* 2 vols. Boston: Houghton Mifflin, 1887.

   Emerson, Edward Waldo. *Emerson in Concord: A Memoir, Written for the "Social Circle" in Concord.* Detroit: Gale Research Company, 1970. (Reprint of early biography by Ralph Waldo Emerson's son.)

   Richardson, Robert D. *Emerson: The Mind on Fire.* Berkeley: University of California Press, 1995.

   Rusk, Ralph Leslie. *The Life of Ralph Waldo Emerson.* New York: Scribner, 1949.

Emerson, William. *Diaries and Letters of William Emerson, 1743-1776, Minister of the Church in Concord, Chaplain of the Revolutionary Army.* Ed. Amelia Forbes Emerson. N.p.: Privately published, 1972.

Fischer, David Hackett. *Paul Revere's Ride.* New York: Oxford University Press, 1994.

French, Allen. *The Day of Lexington and Concord: The Nineteenth of April, 1775.* Boston: Little, Brown, 1925.

————*The First Year of the American Revolution.* Boston: Houghton Mifflin, 1934.

————*Old Concord.* Boston: Little, Brown, 1915.

Garrelick, Renee. *Clothier of the Assabet: The Mill and Town of Edward Carver Damon.* Concord: R. Garrelick, 1988.

————*Concord in the Days of Strawberries and Streetcars.* Concord: Town of Concord, 2006.

Gross, Robert A. *The Minutemen and Their World.* New York: Hill and Wang, 2001. (A standard work, first published in 1976.)

Hawthorne, Nathaniel. *The American Notebooks.* Ed. Randall Stewart. New Haven: Yale University Press, 1932.

————*The Blithedale Romance.* Ed. Seymour Gross and Rosalie Murphy. New York: Norton, 1978.

————*The Centenary Edition of the Works of Nathaniel Hawthorne.* Columbus: Ohio State University Press, 1963-present. (The definitive scholarly edition.)

————*The Hawthorne Treasury: Complete Novels and Selected Tales of Nathaniel Hawthorne.* Ed. Norman Holmes Pearson. New York: Modern Library, 1999.

————*The House of the Seven Gables.* Ed. Robert S. Levine. 2nd ed. New York: Norton, 2005.

————*Nathaniel Hawthorne's Tales: Authoritative Texts, Backgrounds, Criticism.* Ed. James McIntosh. New York: Norton, 1987.

————*The Scarlet Letter and Other Writings.* Ed. Leland S. Person. 4th ed., rev. New York: Norton, 2004.

————*Selected Letters of Nathaniel Hawthorne.* Ed. Joel Myerson. Columbus: Ohio State University Press, 2002.

————*Tales and Sketches.* New York: Library of America, 1996.

About:

Hawthorne, Julian. *Nathaniel Hawthorne and His Wife: A Biography.* 2 vols. Hamden, Connecticut: Archon Books, 1968. (Reprint of early biography by the Hawthornes' son.)

Marshall, Megan. *The Peabody Sisters: Three Women Who Ignited American Romanticism.* Boston: Houghton Mifflin, 2005.

McFarland, Philip. *Hawthorne in Concord.* New York: Grove Press, 2004.

Mellow, James R. *Nathaniel Hawthorne in His Times.* Baltimore: Johns Hopkins University Press, 1998. (First published in 1980; still unsurpassed as a comprehensive biography of Hawthorne.)

Wineapple, Brenda. *Hawthorne: A Life.* New York: Random House, 2004.

Hudson, Charles. *History of the Town of Lexington, Middlesex County, Massachusetts, from Its First Settlement to 1868.* 2 vols. Boston: Houghton Mifflin, 1913.

Jarvis, Edward. *Traditions and Reminiscences of Concord, Massachusetts, 1779–1878.* Ed. Sarah Chapin. Amherst: University of Massachusetts Press, 1993.

Kehoe, Vincent J.-R., comp. *"We Were There!": April 19th, 1775.* 2 vols. Chelmford, Massachusetts: The compiler, 1974. (Consists of first-hand accounts of the Lexington and Concord Fights. The first volume is subtitled "The British Soldiers," the second "The American Rebels.")

Lemire, Elise. *Black Walden: Slavery and Its Aftermath in Concord, Massachusetts.* Philadelphia: University of Pennsylvania Press, 2009.

Lexington (Mass.). *Proceedings at the Centennial Celebration of the Battle of Lexington, April 19, 1875.* Lexington: The Town, 1875.

The Lexington-Concord Battle Road. Concord: Concord Chamber of Commerce, 1975.

Lexington Historical Society. *Proceedings of the Lexington Historical Society, and Papers Relating to the History of the Town, Read by Some of Its Members.* 4 vols. Lexington: The Society, 1890–1912. (Papers on a variety of Lexington-related subjects, including "A Sketch of the History of Lexington Common," "Captain John Parker," "The Old Taverns of Lexington," "The Military Organizations of Lexington," "The Epitaphs in the Burying-Grounds," "Clock-Making in Lexington," "How the Hancock-Clarke House Was Saved," "The Munroe Tavern," "The Rev. Jonas Clarke, Minister and Patriot," and "Extracts from Letter of Miss Betty Clarke, Daughter of Rev. Jonas Clarke.")

Little, David B. *America's First Centennial Celebration: The Nineteenth of April 1875 at Lexington and Concord, Massachusetts.* Boston: Club of Odd Volumes, 1961.

Maynard, W. Barksdale. *Walden Pond: A History.* New York: Oxford University Press, 2004.

Myerson, Joel, ed. *Transcendentalism: A Reader.* New York: Oxford University Press, 2000. (An extensive collection of primary texts.)

Murdock, Harold. *The Nineteenth of April 1775. Exhibiting a Fair and Impartial Account of the Engagement fought on that day, chiefly in the Towns of Concord, Lexington, and Menotomy . . .* Boston: Houghton Mifflin (Riverside Press), 1923.

The Oxford Handbook of Transcendentalism. Ed. Joel Myerson, Sandra Harbert Petrulionis, and Laura Dasson Walls. New York: Oxford University Press, 2010.

Peckham, Alford S. *Lexington: Gateway to Freedom. A pictorial panorama of our heritage.* Lexington: Lexington Chamber of Commerce, 1992.

Petrulionis, Sandra Harbert. *To Set This World Right: The Antislavery Movement in Thoreau's Concord.* Ithaca: Cornell University Press, 2006.

Phinney, Elias. *History of the Battle at Lexington, on the Morning of the 19th April, 1775.* Boston: Printed by Phelps and Farnham, 1825.

Richardson, Laurence Eaton. *The Cannon in Concord: The Concord Independent Battery*. Concord: The Battery, 1973.

———*Concord River*. Barre, Massachusetts: Barre Publishers, 1964.

Ripley, Ezra. *A History of the Fight at Concord, on the 19th of April, 1775, with a Particular Account of the Military Operations and Interesting Events of That Ever Memorable Day; Showing That Then and There the First Regular and Forcible Resistance Was Made to the British Soldiery, and the First British Blood Was Shed by Armed Americans, and the Revolutionary War Thus Commenced*. Concord: Allen & Atwill, 1827.

Robbins, Roland Wells. *Discovery at Walden*. Stoneham, Mass: Printed by George R. Barnstead, 1947. (Reprinted in 1970 by the Thoreau Foundation.)

Ryan, D. Michael. *Concord and the Dawn of Revolution: The Hidden Truths*. Charleston, South Carolina: History Press, 2007.

Scudder, Townsend. *Concord: American Town*. Boston: Little, Brown, 1947. (This readable—although occasionally unreliable—book deals with Concord history through World War II.)

Shattuck, Lemuel. *A History of the Town of Concord; Middlesex County, Massachusetts, from Its Earliest Settlement to 1832; and of the Adjoining Towns, Bedford, Acton, Lincoln, and Carlisle*. Boston: Russell, Odiorne; Concord: John Stacy, 1835. (The first comprehensive history of Concord, still valuable for research.)

Social Circle in Concord. *Memoirs of Members of the Social Circle in Concord*. 7 vols. to date. Concord: The Social Circle, 1882-2005. (Biographies of prominent Concordians from the late eighteenth century to the present time. First volume titled *The Centennial of the Social Circle in Concord*. Second volume includes book-length memoir of Ralph Waldo Emerson by his son, Edward Waldo Emerson, also published separately under title *Emerson in Concord*.)

Teele, John Whittemore, ed. *The Meeting House on the Green: A History of the First Parish in Concord and Its Church. 350th Anniversary, 1635–1985*. Concord: The Parish, 1985.

Thoreau, Henry David. *Collected Essays and Poems*. Ed. Elizabeth Hall Witherell. New York: Library of America, 2001.

———*Familiar Letters of Henry David Thoreau*. Ed. Franklin Benjamin Sanborn. Boston: Houghton Mifflin, 1894.

———*I to Myself: An Annotated Selection from the Journal of Henry D. Thoreau*. Ed. Jeffrey S. Cramer. New Haven: Yale University Press, 2007.

———*Walden, Civil Disobedience, and Other Writings*. Ed. William Rossi. 3rd ed. New York: Norton, 2007.

———*Letters to a Spiritual Seeker*. Ed. Bradley P. Dean. New York: Norton, 2004.

————*A Week on the Concord and Merrimack Rivers, Walden; or, Life in the Woods, The Maine Woods, Cape Cod.* New York: Library of America, 1985.

————*The Writings of Henry D. Thoreau.* Princeton: Princeton University Press, 1971-present. (The definite scholarly edition, superseding the 1906 edition published by Houghton Mifflin.)

> About:
>
> Emerson, Edward Waldo. *Henry Thoreau as Remembered by a Young Friend.* Concord: Thoreau Foundation, 1968. (Reprint of 1917 edition.)
>
> Harding, Walter R. *The Days of Henry Thoreau.* Princeton: Princeton University Press, 1992.
>
> Richardson, Robert D. *Henry Thoreau: A Life of the Mind.* Berkeley: University of California Press, 1986.
>
> Salt, Henry Stephens. *Life of Henry David Thoreau.* Ed. George Hendrick, Willene Hendrick, and Fritz Oehlschlaeger. Urbana: University of Illinois Press, 1993. (A recent edition of an important early biography.)

Tourtellot, Arthur Bernon. *William Diamond's Drum: The Beginning of the War of the American Revolution.* New York: Doubleday, 1959. (Later published under the title *Lexington and Concord: The Beginning of the War of the American Revolution.)*

United States. Boston National Historic Sites Commission. *Final Report of the Boston National Historic Sites Commission.* Washington: G.P.O., 1961.

Walcott, Charles Hosmer. *Concord in the Colonial Period: Being a History of the Town of Concord, Massachusetts from the Earliest Settlement to the Overthrow of the Andros Government, 1635–1689.* Boston: Estes and Lauriat, 1884.

Wheeler, Joseph C. *Ruth Robinson Wheeler: A Concord Life.* Concord: Concord Free Public Library, 2008.

Wheeler, Marian, comp. *Old Burying Grounds of Concord.* Concord: Concord Historical Commission, 1999.

Wheeler, Ruth Robinson. *Concord: Climate for Freedom.* Concord: Concord Antiquarian Society, 1967.

————*Our American Mile.* Concord: Concord Antiquarian Society, 1957.

Wilson, Leslie Perrin. *In History's Embrace: Past and Present in Concord, Massachusetts.* Hollis, New Hampshire: Hollis Publishing, 2007.

Worthen, Edwin B. *Tracing the Past in Lexington, Massachusetts.* New York: Vantage Press, 1998.

ACKNOWLEDGMENTS (2010 PRINTING)

IT'S A SOURCE OF GREAT PLEASURE to everyone connected with the Concord Free Public Library to offer this new edition of *Historic Concord* as a 375th birthday present to the town. This gift is possible only because many people have contributed talent and resources to it. The Friends of the Concord Free Public Library were inspiring in their determination to republish the book and generous in their support. Sherry F. Litwack—a Library Trustee and member of the Friends— was an enthusiastic and energetic co-conspirator and a first-rate organizer from start to finish. Barbara A. Powell—former Director of the Concord Free Public Library—offered me the project of rewriting the guide and allowed ample time for accomplishing the task. Kerry Cronin, Library Director since August 2009, honored the prior commitment of my hours as the work neared completion. The skills of Constance Manoli-Skocay and Robert C. Hall—my staff in the William Munroe Special Collections—were integral to many aspects of the preparation process. The Concord Free Public Library Corporation generously gave permission for the inclusion of historical images from the Special Collections.

I am grateful to members of the Concord and Lexington historical communities who read the near-final version of the manuscript and offered substantive comments for its improvement. My thanks especially to Jayne Gordon, Richard Kollen, D. Michael Ryan, Melissa Saalfield, Joseph C. Wheeler, David Wood, and Joyce T. Woodman.

Library volunteer Elaine Adams created the electronic file for the Allen French history section of the book. Reed Anthony, Bette Aschaffenburg, Carol Gannon, and James Stoessel proofread parts of the manuscript at several points along the way. Ace proofreader Martha Proctor read the final set of proofs. The efforts of project manager/designer Christine Reynolds, mapmaker Leslie Evans, and the Puritan Press have all contributed to the aesthetic appeal and usefulness of the final product.

Last but not least, thanks to the community of Concord for providing a ready-made audience—both interested and well-informed— for this new anniversary edition of *Historic Concord*. —*LPW*

INDEX

boldface = image